THE KIDS
THE BUILDINGS

J.A.LOGGIE

Published in 2015
by J.A. Loggie

ISBN: 978-0-9872122-4-5

Interior layout and cover design
by Publicious Pty Ltd
www.publicious.com.au

Dedication

This book is dedicated to the many hundreds of children who lived in the blocks of flats on Sumner Road Housing Estate in heavily bombed Peckham during the Second World War. This book is also dedicated to the gentle musician who pleaded in vain with a deaf humanity to "… give peace a chance."

Acknowledgements

Publication would not have happened without the encouragement of friends and family. A special thank you goes to Pat Noad, the Queensland author of the Annie Bryce Mysteries, for coaxing the 'Kids' out of the bottom drawer of my desk into the light of day.

Gratitude also to Doug Loggie for his endless patience and time spent teaching an old dog new tricks that enabled her to exchange a quill pen for a computer.

Many thanks and much love to talented Stefanie Jane for her support and the generous contribution of an early e-book cover…stefaniejane.creative@gmail.com

CONTENTS

Introduction

Many emotional stories are told in books and television documentaries about 3,000,000 British children evacuated from densely populated areas in the U.K. in World War Two by the British Government but little is known about the children from families that refused to put their children into the hands of total strangers. This episodic book tells of events in the lives of three children who lived on a social housing estate in heavily bombed Peckham throughout W.W.2. and the reader will see a rarely seen facet of World War Two through their eyes.

London County Council built social housing estates in working-class areas of London in the 1930s under the mantle of 'slum clearance' and the first children to live in the blocks of cramped flats were often labelled the 'kids from the buildings'. Out of consideration for the living and respect for the dead the book's three young protagonists are composites of 'kids from the buildings' well-known to the author.

Nell Smith, Kathy Henson and Mick Doherty were inseparable friends. They were born in a working-class enclave in Vauxhall Street Lambeth on the same September day in 1931 and shortly before the outbreak of W.W.2. their families were evicted from their terraced houses in Vauxhall Street and moved into flats on a new social housing estate in Peckham. The factual bones of their stories are fleshed with just a smidgen of fiction. During the war they slept in the estate's communal air-raid shelters. Bombs often cut water and power supplies and disrupted schooling. They witnessed the Second Great Fire of London in the Blitz and named pilotless V.1 rockets buzz-bombs and doodle-bugs but they never coined a name for the ancestor of todays' ships to the stars the fearsome V2. They were unafraid because they held the child's belief that they were immortal. There was no intent to trivialise the obscenity of war in the lighter hearted tales...children find magic and fun in the darkest of days.

An aged Nell Smith is the book's narrator.

1

Nell Smith begins at the beginning

I was home birthed on the same misty September day in 1931 as my two dearest friends Kathy Henson and Mick Doherty. Our families lived in three adjoining terraced houses in Vauxhall Street, Lambeth. Mick came bellowing into the world at sunrise, I arrived sensibly at noon and gentle diminutive Kathy quietly joined us at sunset. The tired midwife who had worked for hours between three homes to usher a trio of small souls safely into a world in the grip of a world-wide financial depression predicted that we would grow up closer and dearer to each other than natural siblings – a prediction that came true.

Kathy, Mick and I were born into a working-class enclave a two minute walk from iconic Lambeth Walk and the Thames. The front doors of the terraced houses in Vauxhall Street opened directly on to the pavement and neighbours knew each other. The key to most houses hung on a long string from a nail at the back of the door and was easily retrieved through the brass rectangular slot for letters.

Everyone called me Nell even though I was christened

Ellen Kate Smith by the vicar of St Mary the Less, a small Gothic church that graced Black Prince Road in Lambeth from 1827 until 1967. The lovely old church was thriving in 1962 with a congregation of 230 but despite a strong local protest much loved St Mary the Less was demolished in 1967 to make way for an upmarket residential estate.

The Great Depression of the 1930s generated hardship for unemployed workers but it also inspired unity. In 1932 thousands of desperate men walked from Scotland to London on a hunger march and their route was lined every step of the way by sympathetic crowds. My mother and our next-door neighbour Maureen Doherty were among the many housewives who gave the marchers a practical support. The morning the marchers were due to reach Hyde Park Corner my mother and Maureen Doherty loaded their large bassinet prams with buckets of drinking water, boilers of stewed eels taken from the River Thames, loaves of crusty bread baked by our neighbours and tasty cold faggots donated by the local butcher.

Leaving 12 months old Mick and me in our fathers' tender care our mothers wheeled our big bassinet prams across Vauxhall Bridge and walked along Vauxhall Bridge Road towards Hyde Park until they reached an intersection with the marchers' route and in defiance of a troop of mounted police they gave some of the weary men from the North sustenance.

Our mothers came home proud and triumphant that day in spite of their cuts and bruises and the loss of one of Maureen's lace-up boots in a scuffle with a trooper's horse.

My mother died after a short illness in the winter of 1936 when I was five years old and because my father was a night-worker a foster home loomed for me until Maureen and Sean Doherty came to my rescue and for the next two years I slept with the family next door for six nights of the week. Maureen Doherty taught me to cook and how to shop wisely so that by the ripe old age of seven years I was able to cook and shop for myself and my father and if I needed help Maureen was on hand next door.

Manual workers were in the lowest socio-economic strata of the class system that existed in Britain at that time and a bureaucratic plan to replace entire streets of terraced houses in less affluent areas of London with blocks of flats on social housing estates was lauded by the wealthy as the sensible economic solution to a growing lack of inner-city real estate and the Council owned terraced houses in Vauxhall Street that had been occupied by generations of workers' families since the early 1800s were scheduled to be demolished by Council and the evicted tenants rehoused in flats on a new medium-rise housing estate in nearby Peckham.

The towering housing estates that feature in many U.K. television crime dramas were built post-World War Two when lifts became economically viable.

A death-knell sounded for the close-knit community of Vauxhall Street when the London County Council served the first eviction notices. Affordable rental housing in inner London was non-existent in the 1930s and few of the evicted families had any other option than to rent a flat on the newly built Sumner Road Social Housing Estate in nearby Peckham.

Sean Doherty died in 1938 in a tragic work accident on the East India docks one week after the birth of his daughter Teresa and Maureen Doherty faced eviction with two young sons, a new born baby and an aged mother-in-law.

My father escorted Maureen and baby Teresa on a tram to Peckham to inspect the social housing flats. Maureen was dismayed by the small size of the rooms but Dad was concerned by the extent of the estate that began opposite the Sumner Road School and filled the area bounded by Sumner Road, Lisford Street and a canal. On the other side of Lisford Street the uniform brick buildings marched in close-order down both sides of Sumner Road all the way to Commercial Way. The blocks of flats were identical. Four long balconies gave access to the upper level flats but there were no lifts and eight flights of stone stairs had to be climbed to reach the flats on the top balcony. The height of each brick building was identical but the width varied with the number of flats and each building had a bitumen coated courtyard called the 'square'. Household rubbish was placed into a vent on each balcony to drop down a brick chute into an enclosed collection bin in the square. One flat in each building served as a communal laundry with no doors or windows, cold water taps over long concrete sinks on concrete flooring and wire clothes-lines. Maureen expressed heart-felt relief that a Dutch-boy bag-wash laundry was within walking distance in Commercial Way.

The flats had one, two, or three bedrooms. Dad and Maureen had inspected a flat with two bedrooms. The front-door opened on a short passage with a bathroom on the right and a toilet on the left. Crammed inside a small scullery that was also on the left side of the passage was a large coal fired stone boiler for heating water, a gas-stove, a shallow built-in cupboard and a deep kitchen sink underneath a small window that overlooked the long balcony outside.

Between the two small bedrooms at the end of the short passage was a slightly larger room with an open fireplace that the housing officer called the front-room. A large built in wooden coal-box was in the passage outside the door of the front-room.

Dad qualified for a two-bedroom flat and when he saw the size of the rooms he knew that he would have to dispose of most of our furniture from Vauxhall Street although he did hope to squeeze a card table and two kitchen stools into the small scullery.

Maureen believed that children needed to be raised by a community and she believed the gardenless flats would isolate families. Maureen's concerns multiplied when she read the list of Council rules for tenants and discovered that all grassed areas on the housing estate were fenced and off-limits to children and that a bird in a cage was the only pet permitted.

Maureen voiced a dire prediction that children growing up on the new housing estates would become anti-social teenagers unless drastic changes were made by the planners and when Gran Doherty heard that every block of flats on the estate was named for a beautiful tourist spot in the U.K. she grunted that she would be living in 'somewhere else' buildings.

The lack of lifts in the estate troubled adults but it was the pet ban that upset the children. I cried when I gave my Tommy to a friend with a tiny graden but a tortoise needs grass and a patch of earth. The Doherty's fat wheezy bulldog found a good home in the Black Prince pub on Black Prince Road. The publican hoped fierce looking Bitzer would deter thieves but the big ugly dog was actually a friendly slobbery softie. We thought that Bitzer and the publican were suited in looks and nature. No matter how hard we tried we couldn't find a home for Kathy's old cat. Miss Tibbles was arthritic, partially blind and incontinent. Eventually Kathy tearfully agreed, albeit under duress, to allow the vet who looked after the milkman's horse put Miss Tibbles painlessly to sleep and Kathy insisted on holding Miss Tibbles during the mercy euthanasia. Mick and I sat close on each side of Kathy while she tearfully eased her pet's departure.

Miss Tibbles had a grand funeral in the Henson's backyard. Kathy's father dug the grave and Mick's older brother Danny made a wooden cross on which Kathy painted a tiny kitten playing with butterflies. Friends still living in Vauxhall Street came to Miss Tibbles funeral.

Bitzer and Miss Tibbles had been good chums since they were a pup and a kitten and the publican of the Black Prince pub allowed Bitzer to attend the funeral in Mick's custody and one of the barmaids tied a big black velvet bow on Bitzer's new spiked collar.

Gran Doherty sewed long mourning veils from a black muslin underskirt for Kathy and me and advised us to wail loudly if we wanted to give Miss Tibbles a proper Irish wake.

Everybody wailed when Mick spaded earth on top of the white shoe-box coffin and when Danny played Kathy's favourite hymn "All Things Bright and Beautiful" on his mouth-organ we all sang. Bitzer howled until the music stopped. Afterwards Gran Doherty kissed and hugged Kathy and said that Miss Tibbles' funeral was the nicest that she had ever attended.

When the mourners had gone, Kathy, Mick and I knelt and held hands over Miss Tibbles' grave and we swore an unbreakable secret vow. We were going to run away and join a band of gypsies if our adults tried to split us up when we moved to the flats in Peckham.

Happily for some unsuspecting Romany tribe the Smith, Henson, and Doherty families were housed in neighbouring blocks of flats on Sumner Road Social Housing Estate.

2

1938-1939
kids from the buildings in war

A week after Miss Tibbles' funeral Dad and I moved into a two-bedroom flat on the top balcony of Bude House, a block of fifty flats on the corner of Lisford Street and Sumner Road diagonally opposite a small family pub called The *Alliance*.

Kathy and Mick moved into the block of flats on the opposite corner of Sumner Road and Lisford Street. Their building accommodated over a hundred families and was twice as wide as Bude House.

The Bude House balconies and square faced small terraced houses in Jocelyn Street. The entrance to Kathy and Mick's large square faced the *Alliance* pub and small terraced houses in Lisford Street.

Lifts were deemed an unnecessary luxury on the early social housing estates and ground and first floor flats in the five storied buildings were reserved for the elderly and the infirm. Maureen Doherty had two young sons and a baby but it was old Gran her mother-in-law who qualified her family for a three-bedroom ground-floor flat. Kathy was an only child and the

Henson's two-bedroom flat was on the top balcony of the wide building.

Initially I found the view of Tower Bridge seen across a panorama of smoky chimney pots worth a climb of eight flights of stairs to the top of Bude House. I lost all interest in the vista of Tower Bridge on the day Dad decided I was big enough to carry my own bicycle up the stairs on my shoulder.

The stairs on Sumner Road Housing Estate severely tested the stamina of both tenants and visitors. Mothers carried their small children as well as prams and shopping up the stairs. The War Office soon had young fit men wearing a uniform and the elderly and the unfit were left to handle the stairs on the new housing estates. Sooty-faced coalmen, their clothing black and stiff with coaldust, grunted rhythmically as they toiled up the stairs with heavy sacks of coal on their bowed backs to fuel the tenant's open coal fires in wintertime. Central heating was decades away in the future.

Kathy, Mick and I wasted no time in exploring our new world in what remained of our school holidays. We wanted to begin our exploration at Sumner Road School but padlocks on the playground gates defeated us. We couldn't get inside the small Baptist chapel with a spire that snuggled against the side of the school either. Next-door to the chapel was a newsagency where we bought hard-boiled sweets in a twist of newspaper for a farthing. The newsagent's name was Steve and he and his wife lived in one of the two small terraced houses between the newsagency and the *Alliance* pub on the corner. We first heard ourselves addressed as 'kids from the buildings' in Steve's shop.

When we left the newsagency we crossed Sumner

Road to try-out a large playground the Council had built on black asphalt behind two wide blocks of flats that faced the school. We tried the swings, a see-saw, a round-a-bout and a slippery slide; all constructed from iron to thwart vandalism. The Council's metal playground not only survived the kids from the buildings it came unscathed through five years of bombing – vandals had no chance.

When we tired of the playground we walked along Jocelyn Street to Commercial Way and discovered that the terraced houses in Jocelyn Street shared backyard fences with the terraced houses in the next street which was Stanton Street and there we made the thrilling discovery that the towpath of a narrow canal ran past the back fences of the Stanton Street houses.

The canal flowed from under a small ornate iron bridge on Commercial Way. Dilapidated warehouses lined the opposite bank of the waterway which went past the Stourbridge House flats on the other side of Lisford Street – new territory to be explored another day because we saw a majestic Clydesdale horse with beribboned mane plodding along the tow-path towards us towing a gaily painted barge piled high with planks of wood. The gentle equine giant was led by a big friendly bargee. When we introduced ourselves the bargee told us that his name was Alf and that his horse's name was Hercules. We walked beside Hercules and Alf until the towpath reached six steps that went up to the Stourbridge House square.

Alf cheerfully answered all our questions. He told us that his cargo of wood was destined for Whitton's timberyard in Peckham Hill Street and would be unloaded at Eagle Wharf on the other side of

Stourbridge House. We learned that the canal was the Peckham Offshoot of the Grand Surrey Canal and the off-shoot ended at Eagle Wharf because the old time canal builders had run out of money by the time they reached Peckham.

When we finally returned home and told Maureen Doherty about our exciting day she was horrified by the news of a canal so close to adventurous Mick who couldn't swim. Maureen immediately declared the waterway off limits but Mick's mother was a pragmatist and I have no doubt that Maureen prayed every night that none of us would fall into the canal.

We celebrated our eighth birthdays with a noisy combined party in the Doherty's flat and in the middle of a boisterous game of Musical Chairs Danny stopped playing his mouth organ and yelled for silence. Gran turned the sound volume knob on the wireless and we listened in silence to Prime Minister Chamberlain solemnly announce that Britain was at war. Our world was about to turn topsy-turvy again.

3

1939-1940

rules of war and the Dark Maze of Horror

We missed Vauxhall Street and our tiny back yard gardens. Sumner Road Housing Estate was a barren world of bricks and black asphalt where everything living and green had been sacrificed on the altar of bureaucratic economic expediency.

A solitary London Plane tree growing in the centre of Bude House square was a survivor from the eradication of hundreds of family homes and gardens. The tall tree seemed to be a green gift left for us by an unknown architect. The tree's trunk soared up out of black asphalt that covered the Bude House square until the bushy head was level with the top balcony and sparrows and pigeons were crowded on the leafy branches.

When we first saw the plane tree it was untouchable inside a circle of unclimbable tall iron spears until war was declared and the War Office commandeered every scrap of public metal deemed not essential for civilian life and workmen drove a lorry into Bude House square and dismantled the fence of iron spears around the tree.

Mick begged the workmen to give him a spear so that he could be armed to fight the anticipated invasion. The sympathetic workmen explained to eight-year old Mick that every inch of the iron fence was needed to make bullets and tanks for the army.

Kathy, Mick and I were formidable as a combined force and we successfully staked our claim to the tree in Bude House square. When the iron fence was removed our hands could touch the tree's rough bark and with the primal instincts of the young we felt the life-force that pulsates throughout living Earth. We shared our secrets and hatched mischief beneath the tree's leafy canopy. We fed crumbs to the birds that nested on branches among soot grimed leaves until some became so tame they would fly down to us when we whistled for them. Without a garden and forbidden to step on the Council's grass or own a pet the kids from the buildings had no contact with Nature and it seemed reasonable at eight years of age for us to regard the London Plane Tree in Bude House square as a sentient being and our tall green friend was mentioned in our nightly prayers along with our loved ones.

For differing reasons Kathy, Mick and I enjoyed a greater freedom of movement than most of our peers. My father was older than many of my friends' fathers and he worked as a night watchman because he needed the support of a stout stick to walk. Dad had been a soldier in the First World War and his left leg had been crushed under a gun carriage in France.

When I was five years old and my mother died Maureen Doherty had come to my rescue and saved me from foster care. Maureen Doherty had helped raise me so that when war came Dad had an independent eight year old daughter who could manage a household budget with ration books and do her share of the housework and cooking. The key to our front-door hung like a necklace on a string around my neck.

Kathy's front door key also hung on a string around her neck. Kathy's marine commando father was fighting overseas and her mother had returned to her work as a hostess in a club for servicemen and Gloria Henson often came home too late to cook but luckily Maureen Doherty had also kept a motherly eye on Kathy as well as me.

When enemy air-raids increased in 1940 Maureen set a few rules to keep us safe and curb our wandering. She conferred with my father about me and as Gloria Henson was too busy to be bothered by her daughter's activities Maureen included Kathy in her four rules of war.

We had no problem with the first rule that we go everywhere as a threesome – that was what we had always done anyway. The second rule was that Kathy and I had to sleep on a mattress on the floor in Maureen's front room on the nights when Kathy's mother and my father were working. The third rule was that Kathy, Mick and I stayed close to an air-raid shelter at all times. The fourth rule to be home before dark was Maureen's strictest rule but in wintertime the sun set so early that rule four was the most difficult rule to keep. Maureen also made us swear by the 'cross your heart and hope to die' ritual that if the Alert siren sounded during the Saturday morning children's picture show at the Odeon cinema on Peckham High Street we would obey the usherette's orders without giving her any cheek.

We obeyed rules one and two and the Odeon rule but we had promised to keep rules three and four with our fingers crossed behind our backs because we knew that we might have to occasionally bend rules three and four – just a tad.

In anticipation of squadrons of enemy planes raining bombs on Peckham a narrow twisting tunnel with several cul-de-sac off-shoots was excavated under the Bude House square during the first weeks of the war. The hastily dug shelter was reminiscent of an old-time goldmine with a dirt floor and an open entrance at each end. The low roof and the earthen walls were shored up with wooden planks and air inside the underground labyrinth always smelled sour and musty despite the brick air-shafts that poked up into the square. Bude House tenants were unanimous in their refusal to enter the lightless complex underneath their square.

Fortunately by the time the Blitz began the large communal shelters had been built on the stretches of grass on Sumner Road behind the blocks of flats.

Young entrepreneurs living in Bude House did not allow the lightless dank tunnels under the square to go to waste. Kenny Hopkins and his chums peopled the tunnels with mummies and monsters and hung squishy things from the roof. Kenny charged customers a half-penny for an escorted walk with a creepy commentary through the Dark Maze of Horror and only a farthing if you walked alone without a torch.

Kathy, Mick and I partedwith a farthing but we didn't find the Dark Maze of Horror scary Kenny made his four year old brother creep through the dark tunnels wrapped in a dirty white sheet with black crayon around his eyes but Kenny soon stopped that trick when Kathy dried his little brother's tears and threatened to tell Mrs Hopkins on him.

4

1940
boating on the Grand Surrey canal

Paddy Kelly came into our lives a few days after the first enemy bombs fell on London in August 1940. Mick had spotted a broken bassinet pram in the ruins of a bombed house. Of course Mick didn't see a bomb damaged baby carriage Mick saw a fighting ship of the line that he could sail up the Peckham Branch of the Grand Surrey Canal to the Thames.

Unable to dissuade the would-be naval hero Kathy and I assisted in the transportation of his fighting ship to the canal tow-path and we even offered to help him launch his ungainly vessel but we refused to sign on as crew and not even the name H.M.S. Kathy-Nell chalked in large letters on both sides of the big pram could persuade us.

Kathy and I held our breath when Mick gingerly climbed into the big bassinet pram and the H.M.S Kathy-Nell rocked wildly under his weight. Using two flat lengths of wood as oars Mick rowed his ship into the deep water channel in the middle of the canal.

Kathy and I walked along the towpath to monitor

the progress of Mick's unorthodox craft which began to ride dangerously low in the water and we called out encouraging if unhelpful advice to him. The bassinet pram-boat was half-way underneath the Commercial Way Bridge when we heard Mick yell that his ship was taking water.

In the reflected greenish light underneath the bridge we saw that H.M.S Kathy-Nell was indeed sinking fast and Mick was shoulder deep in rising canal water. We called to him in our big sister voices and we calmly advised him to abandon ship and dog-paddle to the shallows at the edge of the towpath and that we would pull him out of the canal but then Kathy and I panicked when Mick yelled, 'I can't – me bleedin' leg's jammed – get someone quick before I drown – get anybody.'

Kathy and I spun about so fast that our faces bumped into the chest of an old man who had come out of one of the Stanton Street backyards and was standing close behind us. Kathy stopped screaming when the old man smiled at her and said softly, 'hush little one, don't be frightened...I'm a friend.'

The stranger was at least as old as Gran Doherty. He had kind blue eyes, a bushy white beard and an Irish accent. He shouted to Mick, 'try to keep your face out of the dirty canal water, Captain – help is on the way.'

The only part of Mick that was showing was his head when the old man shuffled off his shirt and cardigan and kicked off his worn slippers. He sat down on the edge of the towpath and as he eased himself down into the canal water I heard him mutter into his bushy beard, 'by the living saints what was the foolish boyo thinking? Not even the stupid fish swim in this sewer.'

Mick's rescuer dog-paddled out to the middle of the canal and said something encouraging to Mick before he went under the water and extricated Mick's foot from the submerged pram. He was smiling as he listened to Kathy and me roundly scolding Mick while we dragged him out of the canal on to the towpath. When peace was restored the stranger introduced himself, 'my name is Paddy Kelly and what might your names be?'

Kathy gave him a shy sweet smile with her name, 'I'm Kathy Henson.' Kathy grimaced in disgust at a smelly green slime coating Mick's red curls, 'the stinky twerp you saved from drowning in the canal is Mick Doherty.'

'I'm Nell Smith,' I cautiously volunteered to a stranger...a hero but still a stranger.

Paddy Kelly nodded, 'a pleasure to meet all of you I'm sure but now I'm thinking that the Captain's mother should not be seeing her boy looking and smelling like a half-drowned wharf rat. The back yard of my lodgings is a short step back along the towpath and a garden hose and a dry towel may help to minimise his poor mother's shock.'

Mick gratefully accepted the offer and we followed our new friend into the backyard of a Stanton Street lodging house. Paddy attached a hose to a garden tap before he went inside to wash away the smelly canal slime and change his clothes. Kathy and I hosed Mick in the tiny backyard until Mick completely lost his sense of humour and wrestled the hose away from us.

Paddy Kelly returned with two towels that were big enough to dry all three of us and he loaned Mick a patched dressing gown to wear while Mick's shorts and shirt were dripping to wearable dampness on the high back fence.

While we waited for Micks' clothes to dry out Kathy and I gave Mick a well-deserved telling off for using a busted pram as a boat but instead of backing us up Paddy Kelly had quoted Ratty in 'Wind in the Willows, "...there is nothing, absolutely nothing half so much worth doing as simply messing about in boats."

This blatant male support had delighted Mick and so infuriated Kathy and me that peace was not restored again until Paddy gave us half a bottle of flat red Tizer to share and some broken biscuits in a tin with the Changing of the Guard painted in bright colours on the lid.

From that day forward Paddy Kelly became our honorary grandfather and we spent hours playing on the canal towpath. Paddy would scrape wild happy tunes on a little wooden fiddle while Kathy, Mick and I sang and capered around him like three demented demons.

When we tired of singing and prancing we would sit with Paddy on the edge of the canal and he would send tiny puffs of fragrant smoke into the air from his small clay pipe while he told us fantastical tales in his lilting Irish voice.We were entranced by Paddy's stories of dark sorcery in green lands where heroes battled wicked wizards and fearsome monsters and were always victorious.

Old Paddy Kelly came into our lives during the start of dark times and we needed to hear every magical word that dear old man uttered – although we didn't for one moment realise that truth at the time.

5

1940-1941
rabbit stew in the Second Great Fire of London

In the autumn of 1940 the Luftwaffe launched a blitzkrieg of strategic non-stop bombing of Britain that lasted until the summer of 1941 and is known historically as 'the Blitz'. Kathy, Mick and I found the months of intense bombing an exciting time, as did most of our peers who had dodged evacuation. Disruption of schooling, outages of power and water supplies, and sleeping in overcrowded communal shelters were all a part of a grand adventure thanks to the child's irrational conviction of immortality.

Every night we were thrilled by a stunning fantasia of brilliant lights and explosions in the crowded sky above our heads. We were mesmerised by the slow descent of strings and nets of multi-coloured flares amid criss-crossing light sabres of searchlights hunting the bombers skulking in the ominous dark-red clouds in the night sky above our heads.

When we emerged from the communal shelter each morning we found familiar streets had been transformed overnight into alien landscapes by rubble from bomb blasted houses, we picked up oddly shaped pieces of warm metal shrapnel that littered the ground around bomb craters and we eagerly competed with each other to collect clumps of glittering foil ribbons dropped by the bomber pilots to confound their detection by radar. The local pubs, clubs and dance-halls used to buy the decorative anti-radar chaff from us.

Kathy and I shared a bunk-bed in a Sumner Road communal shelter during the non-stop night-raids in the Blitz and we slept with the Doherty family under the watchful eyes of Gran and Maureen. Every morning when he came home from work my father would make a brief stop at the shelter and check on me before going up to our flat to try and sleep.

On Sunday morning the 29th of December 1940 my Dad surprised Kathy, Mick and me. We were on school holidays and Monday was Dad's night off work and as a holiday treat he had bought four tickets for Monday's matinee performance of a Christmas pantomime at the New Cross Empire. Kathy and Mick would be visiting the New Cross Empire for the first time and they were over the moon with excitement.

A matinee at the New Cross Empire was my favourite outing, I so loved the plays and the florid melodramas the Empire staged and Dad enjoyed the variety shows and musical revues. Maureen gave her consent for Kathy and Mick to go with Dad to see the pantomime because she trusted him to keep us safe if there was an air-raid alert. The Empire management used to boast that an air-raid had never stopped a show and that the audience always stayed in their seats during a raid because the palatial theatre building was more bomb-proof than the bomb shelters outside on the main road but Dad reckoned that the audiences never heard the Alert sirens or the noise of the bombs and anti-aircraft guns over the Empire's loud music and even louder voice of the Master of Ceremonies.

The Alert sirens wailed a few minutes after Dad had left the shelter to go up to our flat on that fateful Sunday morning and neighbours who left the shelter after breakfast returned in a steady stream with many dramatic stories about burning houses.

We were not allowed to leave the shelter until the All-Clear sirens sounded so we passed time with a new board game called Monopoly that Maureen's seaman brother had bought for his nephews when his ship docked in America. Between Kathy and Mick's excited chatter about the pantomime and my efforts to uncover how Danny was manipulating the dice that decided how many spaces a player moved around the Monopoly board I hardly noticed the fire engine bells outside the shelter.

When the All-Clear sirens wailed after lunch Maureen ordered us to pack our game away because she had work for us. Maureen had been given three plump rabbits by her cousin in the Women's Land Army, a munificent gift in days of stringent food rationing but a problem to cook. Warming the baby's milk bottle and making a hot drink on a small primus stove was acceptable in the crowded poorly ventilated communal shelter but cooking meat was not and for two days in the short breaks between air-raids Maureen had trekked back and forth from her flat to the shelter until she had cooked a large boiler of deliciously tasty rabbit stew.

Maureen gave a specific task to each of us that Sunday. She ordered Danny, Mick and I to accompany her to the Doherty's flat and wait while she re-heated the rabbit stew, then the two boys had to carry the heavy boiler of hot stew between them to the shelter.

If the warning sirens had not sounded I was to take a large jug of hot rabbit stew up to my Dad who by that time would be up and getting dressed to do his two hours of voluntary fire watching for the A.R.P before he went to work.

Kathy had loudly protested at being delegated to remain in the shelter and help Gran look after little Teresa who was never out of mischief now that she was toddling but Mick, Danny and I had supported Maureen's decision. Kathy had weak lungs and she fought for breath whenever there was even a wisp of smoke in the air and according to everyone who came into the shelter that morning the air outside was dense with smoke from burning buildings.

Gran suggested that Kathy wore her gasmask whenever she went outside after an air-raid and Mick and I thought that was an excellent suggestion. Kathy was not keen on Gran's idea.

Maureen, Danny, Mick and I walked into thick choking smoke outside the shelter. The dark acrid smoke stung our eyes and left an unpleasant metallic taste in our mouths and we could hear what sounded like hundreds of fire-engine bells all around us.

While Maureen was reheating the large boiler of rabbit stew the boys and I packed two carrier bags with loaves of bread and slabs of delicious spicy bread pudding that Gran and Maureen had baked. We were going to have a shelter feast.

The dense smoke from burning houses had shortened the winter daylight hours even more and although it was only three o'clock in the afternoon it was dark and I needed the dim light of my blue papered torch when I climbed the stairs to the top balcony of Bude House with a jug of piping hot rabbit stew for my Dad.

I was surprised to find our flat was empty and that my father's bed had not been slept in. I stood the jug of hot stew in the scullery sink and went outside to look out over the balcony.

Several houses were alight in nearby streets and I noticed a man wearing an ARP armband at the far end of my balcony near the second set of Bude House stairs and I walked along the balcony to ask him if he had seen my father. He spoke first, 'hello young lady, I bet that you are Miss Nellie Smith. My name is Bert Miller and I'm an old chum of your Da.'

Bert Miller was roughly about Dad's age, he had a kind wrinkled face and grey hair. He leaned on a heavy walking stick and he spoke with a Liverpool accent.

'I'm very pleased to meet you, Mr Miller. Do you know where my Dad is? He's not in the flat and his bike's missing.'

Bert Miller nodded, 'your Da was called away on an urgent job. Some nearby stables are on fire and there were horses to be saved but don't you worry, your Da will be fine. There ain't a bloke living better able to handle a scared nag than Smithy. I was in his gun-crew in the first stoush in France and I'll never forget the night the barn where we stabled the little mare that pulled our field gun caught fire. There were other horses in the barn that were crazy with terror and your Da told us if we put our jackets over the animal's heads and talked softly to the beasts they would let us lead them outside. Thanks to your Da's advice we saved every horse in that barn. I'll tell him that you were here, now you run back to the shelter lass and on the way past your flat close your front door because you're showing a light.'

There was a dim light in the open doorway of my flat, I had forgotten to switch off the scullery light but fires were burning all around us and I didn't think the faint light from the flat could be seen by a bomber pilot. I stared at Bert Miller's walking stick and wanted to ask if his leg had been hurt by the same gun-carriage that had crushed my father's leg but he was no longer in a mood to chat to me.

'Jerry seems to be set on doing his worst tonight so you'd best run back to the shelter lass before the buggers return – I won't forget to tell your Da that you dropped by and remember to switch off that light before you shut your flat door and get yourself into the shelter.'

Tower Bridge was a black silhouette against a backdrop of dark crimson cloud above the docks. The silvery elephantine barrage balloons floating beneath the fiery clouds had a ruddy tinge and I had an uneasy feeling something bad was about to happen.

Bert Miller was staring up at the glowering dark red sky when he said in an urgent voice, 'Run fast lassie because here comes big trouble.'

I had also heard the throbbing beat of a large bomber formation. An Alert siren wailed tardy warning and hundreds of black planes with white crosses on wings and fuselages came down out of the dark red clouds until they appeared to fill the night-sky. Incendiaries were dropping from the black bombers flying low in a thunderous formation towards the burning docklands. I watched the stick-like fire-bombs raining down on the sea of rooftops in front of me and saw flames erupt wherever the incendiaries landed. I was reminded of Gran's lurid descriptions of the hell-fires she said awaited Mick if he didn't mend his ways.

Bert Miller growled, 'off to the shelter with you lass. When Jerry finishes bashing the hell out of the docks he'll fly back home this way. Do you want me to walk you to the shelter?'

'No thank you Mr Miller I'm not scared and I'm a fast runner.'

'Good girl, just like your Da – he was never afeared.' He gave my head an approving pat. 'Best you bide a while at the bottom of the stairs until you're certain that it is safe to go out in the open and run fast to the shelter.'

'Dad told me that the bottom of our stairs is as safe as the shelter.'

He gave me a little push. 'Run lass there's a UXB warning on the corner of Stanton Street and Commercial Way that's way too close to these fires for my peace of mind.'

UXB was the acronym for an unexploded bomb and a warning sign was posted wherever it was suspected that a UXB had burrowed underground. By the end of November 1940 there were over 3,000 unexploded bombs buried in London waiting to be defused by small teams of incredibly brave bomb disposal soldiers

Tower Bridge was cloaked in dark smoke when I ran along the balcony to switch off the scullery light and as I closed the front door an ear stunning explosion rattled all the windows in Bude House. When I looked over the balcony, a thick pall of smoke obscured the ends of Jocelyn and Stanton Street...the UXB under Stanton Street had exploded.

Over the noise of A.A. guns, explosions and fires I could hear the popping of the mobile pom-pom gun that protected a recently installed searchlight and barrage balloon in Kathy and Mick's big square.

The barrage balloon, the searchlight and especially the mobile gun had attracted a huge interest from the kids living in the building and much to Mick's excited delight a squad of A.T.S gunners manned the pom-pom gun and when the lady soldier in charge of the A.T.S. girls ordered Mick away from the pom-pom gun she did so in such a posh voice that Mick, our ardent royalist, was proudly convinced that he had been told to 'sling his hook' by a member of the royal family.

I was cheered when I saw a handful of Spitfires in camouflage colours with roundels on their wings had arrived and were darting in and out of the bomber formation with their guns spitting fire. The Spitfires were like terriers attacking a horde of rats and I was unable to keep track of the dogfights between the Spitfires and enemy fighter planes that were attempting to protect the slow heavy bombers.

I watched an enemy fighter plane and a flaming barrage balloon spiral down to Earth in a fiery embrace and I crossed my fingers as I hoped the burning balloon and plane fell into the Thames and not on someone's house and it never once crossed my mind that a nine year-old girl should not have been aware of such a terrible possibility.

Bert Miller's loud shout of 'oy!' attracted my attention. He also blew a loud blast on a big whistle for good measure, 'hop it to the shelter Nellie Smith or I'll come along there and give you a good clip over the ear.'

I gave Bert a smile and a quick wave to show I hadn't

taken offence before I ran into the utter blackness of the unlit stairs. Dad had stressed so many times that if I couldn't reach a shelter in an air-raid then the bottom of the stairs was the most safest place in every building so down to the bottom of Bude House stairs was where I headed.

I sat lonely and cold in the middle of an air-raid at the bottom of Bude House's stone stairs and my only wish was that somebody would arrive and tell me that Dad and old Paddy Kelly were both safe...nobody was going to arrive because my father's friend Bert Miller was the only person who knew where I was.

I seriously considered going back up the stairs to the top balcony and talking to Bert but I didn't want to chance a whack over the ear. I was wearing my warm hooded siren-suit and thick woollen gloves but I still shivered with cold when I crept up the first flight of stairs and huddled into a corner of the first landing. I squeezed my eyes tight shut whenever a searing flash lit up the stairs until finally I kept my eyes closed and I began to recite aloud from start to finish my favourite stories from Paddy's repertoire of fantasy tales and before I reached the finish of the story about the twelve sleeping dragons I too was fast asleep.

It was quiet and dark when I woke with a stiff neck after sleeping for hours curled up on the stone floor of the first landing. I was coated with gritty dust and the sharp stink of burnt gunpowder in the air made my eyes water. I also realised that if I didn't run fast up the stairs to my flat that I might wet my knickers – I ran upstairs very fast to my empty flat.

Dad's bed had not been slept in...he had not come home or if he had he missed seeing me asleep on the first landing because he had used the second set of stairs to talk to Bert. When I left the flat the clock on the mantelpiece in the front room showed the time was almost 5am and I knew that I was in big trouble with Maureen.

I waited for a few minutes on the top balcony of Bude House but there was no sign of Bert Miller – he had gone home.

I guessed that I had slept through an All Clear siren because no bombers were raining incendiaries and the pom-pom gun was silent. I looked out towards Tower Bridge and saw that fires still burned in many houses. When I ran down the stairs and stepped out into the square I coughed in the smoke filled air and I cried a little when I saw the hundreds of tiny feathered bodies scattered over the fire-lit asphalt of the square. A lone searchlight beam was probing the dark red sky and I knew that if an enemy was pinpointed then more searchlights would flare into life to enmesh the intruder in a deadly web of lights for the A.A. guns on the ground to destroy.

I walked out of Bude House square in an eerie red light. The noise of guns, planes and explosions had been replaced by fire-engine bells and the loud voices of men fighting fires in the houses at the Commercial Road end of Jocelyn Street, their fire hoses stretched out like long black snakes across the gleaming wet road.

I recalled the tremendous explosion that had rattled the windows in Bude House and the fears caused by the UXB warning sign posted at the end of Stanton Street returned ten-fold. I remembered Paddy telling us that he and the other men in his lodging house preferred to wait out an air-raid in the cellar of the house rather than the small overcrowded Anderson shelter in the garden. The hot water that I was in with Maureen couldn't possibly get any hotter…I decided to check on Paddy in Stanton Street before I returned to the shelter and Maureen.

I was shocked when I saw Stanton Street. The street was choked with bricks and broken masonry, the terraced houses that shared back fences with Jocelyn Street houses were ruined shells and the houses on the canal side of the street had been flattened to rubble.

I heard someone blowing an ARP whistle and shouting but it wasn't Bert Miller. A tall skinny boy rugged up against the frosty air was clambering over the debris in the road he was coming towards me. He wore an armband that marked him as a volunteer messenger and a big whistle hung on a lanyard around his neck.

'Who gave you permission to enter Stanton Street?' he rudely demanded in a loud voice.

'Who gave a messenger-boy permission to question me?' I asked in my snooty voice.

'I'm the officer in charge of looting prevention in Stanton Street. No one enters this street, especially not a kid like you, unless they prove to me that they are a bona fide resident.'

He looked to be only a couple of years older than Mick's brother Danny who was twelve years old, 'how do I know that you're not a looter?' I demanded.

When he lifted his whistle to his lips I thought he was about to summon reinforcements and I quickly changed my attitude and tried to butter him up instead.

'I'm sorry sir, I can see now that you're an important ARP officer. I ain't a looter sir. Mum sent me out to check on our poor old Gran after the fire-bomb raid last night – Gran lives in Stourbridge House flats.'

He hesitated before the whistle dropped and hung on the lanyard, 'go ahead then – but when you get home you tell your mother that the important ARP officer who stopped you will prosecute her if he catches you trying to enter a forbidden zone again.'

'Yes Sir, I'll tell her, Sir – ta ever so much, Sir.'

Aware of him watching I ran along Lisford Street to the Stourbridge House square and in the smoky darkness he didn't see me step aside down the steps to the canal tow-path.

The debris strewn towpath was lit by fires burning in the old warehouses lining the other side of the canal. I could hear the fire-fighters' voices and someone yelled a warning a second before something collapsed. A ball of red sparks flew high over the canal and came down in a red shower of fiery rain that sizzled out on the dark canal water.

An eerie silence descended on the towpath when I picked a careful path through smashed and scattered back fences and before I reached the little iron bridge under which Mick nearly drowned I saw the site of the UXB that vibrated windows in Bude House when it destroyed Stanton Street.

I walked very slowly through broken furniture and personal belongings scattered around the rim of a deep wide crater that yawned where Paddy's lodging house had once stood. I had no idea of what I was looking for until I spotted a biscuit tin with the changing of the guard on the lid. The biscuit tin was partially buried in the dirt and dust of broken bricks and the lid was scratched and dented but a small shake confirmed the presence of biscuits bits inside.

I sat on the edge of the canal in the same spot where Kathy, Mick and I had so often sat with Paddy while he lit our drab world with tales of magic and fantasy. I nursed the dented biscuit tin feeling numb inside unable to cry. I would cry a bucket of tears later with Kathy. Mick wouldn't cry, I've never seen Mick cry. I had concluded a long time ago that yelling bad words instead of crying was the boys' way.

The winter sun was lighting the eastern horizon when I heard a bicycle bell and saw a man wheeling a bicycle through shadowy piles of fire-lit rubble in the street. The man was ringing the bicycle bell as he walked towards me. I suddenly wondered if the man was the snooty boy's ARP boss and I stood up ready to run when a voice I most wanted hear in the whole wide world quietly called my name, 'Nellie! Is that you?'

Dad was safe. When we had stopped laughing and hugging we sat together on the edge of the tow-path. The fire-fighters had put out most of the fires in the warehouses directly facing us across the canal but an occasional shower of red sparks still spluttered out on the surface of the water.

I was shivering with cold and Dad opened wide his coat for me to snuggle against him and he buttoned his badly scorched coat around me as he used to do when I was a little kid and I didn't care that Dad and his coat had a really bad sweaty horse stink.

'Were you very angry when you didn't find me in the shelter?' I asked him.

'Not now that I've found you safe.'

'I bet Maureen is furious. But it wasn't my fault I couldn't get back to the shelter.'

'Maureen thought that you had stayed with me in the flat last night and she became upset when she realised that you were missing, your faithful chums

Kathy and Mick spent the night wrapped in blankets on the shelter floor near the shelter door waiting for you to come home. Where did you sleep last night?'

'I slept on the first landing of Bude House stairs – you said that the stairs were the safest place to be in an air-raid if I couldn't reach a shelter. Maureen had sent me up to our flat with a jug of rabbit stew for you and I met Mr Bert Miller who was on fire-watch on our balcony and he told me that you were rescuing horses from a burning stable and then he yelled at me to run back to the Sumner Road shelter.'

'Why didn't you do as Bert told you and run back to the shelter?'

'I did try to return to the shelter but I didn't get a chance. A big raid started with no siren warning and incendiaries began dropping, Then as I was shutting our front-door the UXB at the end of Stanton Street exploded so I ran down the stairs and waited on the first landing for the All Clear siren but I fell asleep and I didn't wake up until five o'clock this morning.'

I looked at the huge crater where Paddy's lodging-house used to stand and at last I cried.

Dad said quietly, 'I've got news that will dry those tears. A water-main burst in Stanton Street yesterday morning and flooded the basements and Anderson shelters of the houses on the canal side of the street. The W.V.S. ladies found beds in nearby shelters for the residents and that included the boarding house men. I reckon that burst water-main saved hundreds of lives in Stanton Street last night. The UXB flattened empty water-logged houses.'

I was still taking in the unbelievable news when Dad shouted, 'we're over here boys.'

In dawn's dim smoky light I saw Mick and Danny and an ugly small boy in a hooded siren suit climbing over the heaps of debris. The two boys were lifting their companion bodily over the biggest chunks of masonry. When the trio reached us I saw the small boy in the siren suit was Kathy wearing her hated gas-mask.

Kathy, Mick and I were so relieved and happy to be re-united with each other that our group hug would have lasted until the sun came up if Dad hadn't pulled us apart. He smiled down at Kathy in her gasmask and then he looked at Mick and Danny, 'Good morning lads. Where did you find this little Munchkin from Mars?'

'Good morning, Mr Smith,' Mick and Danny chorused and Mick said, 'it's Kathy wearing her gas-mask. Mum wouldn't let her leave the shelter unless she wore her gas-mask because of the smoke.'

Danny grumbled, 'Kathy and Mick refused to stay in the shelter after they heard the news that the UXB in Stanton Street had detonated last night and Mum made me go with them.'

Danny walked to the edge of the huge crater. He stood there staring down for a moment before he said, 'Wow! The old Irish codger must be in a million bits down there…'

Making fierce strange noises inside her gas mask Kathy attacked Danny from the rear with a large piece of wood. Dad quickly intervened and took Kathy's makeshift club away.

'Relax Kathy. I've got some really good news about your friend Mr Kelly.'

When Dad finished explaining about the burst water main Mick and Danny whooped and danced an impromptu jig with me and Kathy. Then when Dad calmed us down Kathy raised her gas-mask so that he could understand what she was saying, 'please Mr Smith, can we go and see Paddy now?'

I joined in, 'I want to to give Paddy his biscuit tin.'

'Later girls – it's still dark. Wait until the sun is a bit higher. I wouldn't mind a big bowl of Maureen's rabbit stew that I've been hearing so much about.'

Kathy said, 'I want to ask Paddy about the tiny red lights on the canal. They look like the magic fairy candles in his story about the leprechauns that always makes Mick laugh.'

'What tiny red lights are you talking about, Munchkin?' Dad asked.

Kathy pointed to the canal, 'the pretty red lights that are floating on the water.'

Everyone turned and stared at the thousands of tiny crimson lights that were floating over the canal towards us. I moved to the edge of the towpath for a closer look and Danny jerked me back by my coat belt and at same time Dad swept Kathy up into his arms and shouted, 'get off the tow-path kids…scarper up to the road as fast as you can!'

We hastily clambered over the heaps of house debris and followed Dad up to the road. He lifted Kathy on to the saddle of his bike and told Mick and Danny to run to Lisford Street wheeling the bike between them and making sure that Kathy didn't fall off.

The boys set off at a run with Kathy on the bike between them and Dad grabbed my hand and didn't stop running with me until we were all standing in Lisford Street.

Kathy, Mick and I asked together, 'what was so scary about those pretty red lights?

Danny shuddered, 'Rats! They're real nasty little sods.'

Dad nodded, 'Danny is right and there must be millions of them in the warehouses and they're swimming across the canal to escape being barbequed. Kathy your pretty red lights were the reflections of the fires in their eyes. They'll soon be squabbling over new nesting places in the ruins of the bomb-blasted houses.'

Dad looked around with a puzzled frown, 'I wonder where young Nigel went. I must warn him about the rats. Nigel's only fifteen but he takes his A.R.P. duties very seriously and he is on looter alert. I'm surprised that he allowed any of you to enter Stanton Street'

I saw a knowing grin flash between Danny and Mick. Then Kathy, who was sitting high on the saddle of the bike, leaned forward and gave Mick's exposed neck a twisty nail-pinch.

'Ouch! What was that for?'

Kathy raised her gasmask and said in her no-nonsense voice, 'Mick, give the messenger boy's property to Mr Smith – right now!'

'I wasn't keeping it,' Mick muttered and with his free hand he handed Dad a whistle on a lanyard. 'He dropped it when he bolted...I can't think why he scarpered...can you Danny?'

Danny was grinning when he said, 'maybe our alien from Mars scared him.'

My father stared thoughtfully at Danny. 'There are too few volunteers for the messenger service so if Nigel resigns tonight I'm sure you won't mind if I talk to Maureen about you doing a spot of volunteer duty for the A.R.P. Daniel Doherty.'

Danny looked alarmed but a faint undulating wail of a far off siren silenced his protest at Dad's threat. The distant wailing became steadily louder as like the hilltop beacon-fires of an England long past, district after district passed on the warning of an approaching enemy.

'The buggers are returning for another go. It's time to shake a leg kids.' Dad quickened his pace and we broke into a trot beside him. 'We might have to miss the pantomime matinee. I think Hitler's Luftwaffe pilots are trying to burn London down.'

Danny grimly laughed and pointed to Paddy's biscuit tin that I was still nursing. 'I don't fancy their chances, not when the bleeders couldn't even blow up an old Irish…his eyes went to Kathy, '…a nice old Irish gentleman's tin of broken biscuit bits.'

Kathy removed her gasmask completely and gave Danny her sweetest smile of approval.

Sunday night the 29th of December 1940 inner London was fire-bombed into a blazing inferno that has become known historically as the 'Second Great Fire of London'.

6

1941
a brief evacuation

In anticipation of bombing raids on the U.K. by a modern well equipped Luftwaffe the British Government activated a Child Evacuation scheme during the first weeks of Britain entering the war and more than 3,000,000 children living in densely populated areas in the U.K. were removed from their homes and sent to live with host families in safer areas.

The evacuation at short notice of so many children was a vast undertaking that was seldom a happy experience for children whose parents could not afford a private evacuation. Siblings were separated and hosted miles away from each other and the parents of the evacuees often waited months to learn where each of their children had been billeted.

Although the evacuation of children was optional the hosting of the Government evacuees was not optional and people living in an area deemed unlikely to be targeted by bombers who had a spare room were fined if they refused to accommodate a Government evacuee. This ruling caused a great deal of resentment that was often deflected on to the already unhappy homesick evacuee. Another cause of friction was the cultural differences that existed between working-class city and country families in the 1930s.

To combat a lack of host families the Children Overseas Reception Board was established in June 1940 and evacuation of children to Church and State institutions in commonwealth countries began. The Children Overseas Reception Board was dismantled after the S.S. City of Benares was torpedoed on route to Canada in September 1940 and seventy-seven of the ninety C.O.R.B. evacuees on board drowned in the Atlantic.

Kathy, Mick and I were fortunate to have been born into a close-knit working-class culture in Lambeth, a culture in which neighbours were viewed as extended family and single parent children and children with a dysfunctional family were protected from harm. Sending young children away from their family to live with strangers in a boarding school was frowned upon by the working-class residents in Vauxhall Street and regarded as an abnegation of parental duty...how elite and how expensive the boarding school was did not impress them.

Families with contacts and relatives outside London opted for a private evacuation of their children but very few of the evicted Vauxhall Street families living in the flats on the Sumner Road Estate signed up for the Government evacuation scheme, the majority chose to keep their children with them during the war.

Maureen had rejected the Government's evacuation scheme as soon as she learned that infants had to be accompanied by a parent and that she would be evacuated with Teresa but her two sons would be split up and billeted with different host families and her mother-in-law also rejected evacuation. Gran completely distrusted the Government after her forced eviction from Lambeth, a distrust shared by many of our neighbours who agreed with Gran when she said to an evacuation officer, 'if the good Lord decides to use a bomb to take us to Heaven then we will go together and meet him as a loving Christian family.'

Maureen also knew she could rely on her eldest son to help care for the rest of the family. Danny was a sensible twelve-year old well on his way to filling his late father's shoes as the man of the family. Days after the first bombs fell on London Maureen invited my Dad and Kathy's parents to her flat to discuss the possible evacuation of Kathy and me over a pot of tea. Kathy's soldier father was on embarkation leave and Maureen wanted to be certain of his wishes for Kathy before he sailed overseas.

Both Kathy's father and my father voted against our evacuation although Gloria Henson argued strongly for Kathy's evacuation. With the exception of Gloria Henson, our adults had finally agreed over the pot of tea in Maureen's flat that distant strangers posed a bigger threat to children than bombs and Gloria Henson had grudgingly acceded to her husband's wish that Kathy remained in Peckham with Mick and me under Maureen Doherty's guidance...at least for the present.

At the end of that week Kathy's marine-commando sailed away to fight the war overseas and we never saw Mr Henson again.

The non-stop day and night air-raids in the Blitz disrupted sleep and schooling and often cut London's water and power supplies for days and the Government

Evacuation officers constantly urged families with children still living at home in bombed areas to accept the Government's offer to evacuate their children. Large posters went on public display with the message that parents who loved and cared for their children evacuated them but I believe it was the head-lice that eventually persuaded Maureen to surrender and give the evacuation scheme a tentative try. Kids in the over-crowded communal shelters on the Sumner Road Estate were sleeping two and three to a bunk and head-lice spread like wildfire.

Maureen Doherty had taken on the role of a loving surrogate mother to Kathy and me in Lambeth and it was with great reluctance that she reluctantly agreed to our trial evacuation with Mick to Lesser Dymwich, a village buried deep in the high hedged lanes of Hampshire but only after she had harassed the evacuation office into giving her an iron clad assurance that we would be hosted close to each other and that she would have our addresses. Maureen also obtained a written assurance from a desperate evacuation officer that Lesser Dymwich was of no interest whatsoever to Herr Adolf Hitler.

During the first week of April 1941 Dad took Kathy, Mick and me to Waterloo Station on a bus and handed us into the care of a W.V.S lady who was to escort us to Lesser Dymwich on a steam train crowded with soldiers embarking overseas. Every soldier on the train had a large kitbag and a long heavy 303. Rifle. Mick was transported to boy Heaven when one of the soldiers sat on the carriage floor with him and showed him how to take a 303. rifle apart for cleaning. Our young pretty escort blushed a deep pink whenever a soldier spoke to her but I rather think she was sorry when we reached our destination and left the crowded train at a large market town where we boarded a country bus that was waiting outside the station. After a bumpy bus ride through narrow leafy lanes the bus-driver deposited us with our gasmasks, our carrier-bags and our escort beside the Lesser Dymwich village green.

None of us had ever travelled so far from London before and we were intrigued by our first sight of story-book cottages with thatched roofs nestled in gardens bright with spring flowers. A grey stone church with a Norman tower topped by a spire overlooked the village green and on the far side of the green was an inn with a faded swinging sign. There didn't appear to be many people in the small shops that were on each side of the inn and one of the shops seemed to be a post-office-cum-grocery store.

'Blimey! Gran wouldn't half grouse about shopping if she saw this lot. Do the ladies in Lesser Dymwich have to catch a bus to another village to shop in a co-op?' Mick asked.

The W.V.S girl smiled at Mick when she shook her head, 'the neighbouring villages are similar to Lesser Dymwich. They all have Dymwich in their name and they all have a village green and the nearest co-op is in the market town where you left the train from London.'

Kathy only had eyes for a big oak tree with wide spread leafy branches growing in the centre of the village green and she asked if there was a big oak-tree growing on every village green and our escort shook her head. 'I know there are shade trees on most of the Dymwich village greens but as far as I can recall Lesser Dymwich has the only oak tree.'

'Why do the villages have a green when every cottage has a garden?' asked puzzled Mick.

'A medieval royal charter gives every Dymwich villager the legal right to graze animals, stage fetes and play games on a piece of common land in the middle of their village and that right is treasured by the locals who know that a lot of fun can be had on a village green.'

Mick looked and sounded doubtful, 'I'm sorry Miss but Lesser Dymwich village green looks about as lively as a graveyard to me – I'm already missing Rye Lane. Where do the village kids go to school? Where is the school?'

'A bus will take you to the local primary school in Upper Dymwich every day. A word of caution, Major Handley-Carr does surprise checks on the school bus so never travel without your gas-mask or your identity card. Don't worry Mick, you'll get used to country life.'

'Who is Major Handley-Carr?' Mick asked.

'He is in charge of the Dymwich Home Guard. The Major conducts air-raid drills and he will teach you about air-raid sirens and what happens in an air-raid.'

Our nice W.V.S lady was consulting her clip-board and missed our baffled expressions.

'Now it's time for you to meet the kind folk who are waiting to welcome you into their homes.'

During our very brief stay in Lesser Dymwich, Mick, whose family was devout Irish Roman Catholic, was billeted with the elderly Anglican vicar the Reverend Molland and his housekeeper Molly. Reverend Molland and Molly didn't have a nasty bone in their bodies and we grew very fond of them. Molly used to bake little biscuit treats especially for us.

Kathy and I were not so lucky with our host, we were

billeted with Miss Drew the acidic commandant of the local Girl Guides. Vinegar Drew lived with three cats on the outskirts of the village in a big house the villagers called the 'manor-house'. Miss Drew's house had five double bedrooms and Kathy and I slept on two narrow camp beds in a small linen-room and we were given household duties to perform before and after school.

When she was first assigned evacuees Miss Drew had complained that she did not want low class London children sleeping under her roof but an evacuation officer had shamed her into hosting me and Kathy. She had paid a refusal fine to avoid hosting Mick.

When Kathy and I arrived on Miss Drew's doorstep she checked our hairs for head lice before she allowed us to step inside the house and then she asked our embarrassed WVS escort if she knew when we had last bathed or indeed if we had ever bathed.

Miss Drew's antipathy made our first weeks in Lesser Dymwich miserable and homesick for London. The new school, different food, a strange dialect and stranger mores of village life were as alien to us as they would have been to pygmies raised in a jungle but we were soon good friends with most of the village children and kindly tolerated by the rest.

Lesser Dymwich in summertime was a ten year old child's paradise. Fragrant wild roses rambled over the tall hedgerows that bordered the network of narrow lanes connecting the villages and succulent wild berries ripened on rampant bramble bushes on the edges of the surrounding green fields. Foxes barked at night and in the daytime dashed streaks of warm brown through the small stands of woodland where bluebells created intense blue carpets and when the sun crept above the horizon the earthy aroma of fresh mushrooms scented the air but exiles see life through a glass darkly and our hearts ached for London's noisy streets.

Mick went out early one morning to pick wild mushrooms for the vicar's breakfast and he met a dark eyed Romany boy also collecting mushrooms. Both boys instantly recognised a fellow outsider and introduced themselves. The gypsy boy's name was Simon and he was ten years old. Mick showed Simon the puckered shrapnel scar on his stomach and as boys will do Simon reciprocated the friendly gesture and took Mick to see a hidden badger-sett in a small wood outside the neighbouring village of Dymwich Meadows.

Simon told Mick that his tribe was camped in a nearby field where they had the owner's permission to camp for two weeks every year then he showed Mick seven brightly painted horse-drawn caravans parked in a close circle around two small camp-fires. Simon's mother was cooking breakfast on one of the campfires and she invited Mick to sit on the grass and enjoy breakfast with Simon. She told Mick that the gypsies camped in the field outside Lesser Dymwich for the same two weeks each year and they earned money working at a large fete held on the Lesser Dymwich village green on the last Saturday in July which happened to be that coming Saturday. Kathy and I were thrilled by the news of the fete but Mick overheard even more exciting news while weeding the flower bed underneath the open window of the vicar's study where the fete committee was holding a meeting. He heard Miss Drew's cold waspish voice say, 'The three London savages will wreck the Hunt. I insist they compete as a team. Keeping an eye on the Unholy Trinity will be easier if it is kept intact.'

When the committee members had gone home a beaming Reverend Molland told Mick that the fete committee had voted to allow evacuees in the villages to join the Dymwich Hunt.

'Sorry Vicar but we don't do hunting. Kathy and Nell would give me a right good ragging if I let a pack of dogs tear a poor little fox to bits,' Mick said.

Reverend Molland laughed, 'no animals are involved Mick – the Hunt is a local tradition that dates back to the civil war between the Roundheads and the Cavaliers. A badly wounded cavalier messenger hid a parchment scroll he was carrying before succumbing to his wounds. Stamped with the royal seal and tied with a purple ribbon the scroll bears the names of every Royalist living in the Dymwich area at that time and has never been found despite the King beheading of the local Royalist squire. Today any child resident within a two mile radius of Lesser Dymwich has the right to search for a hidden replica of the scroll during the annual Dymwich fete, which happens to be this coming Saturday. Miss Drew had insisted that the evacuees in the villages were ineligible to compete because they are temporary residents but she was persuaded to withdrew her opposition to you and Nell and Kathy being part of the Hunt on a strict proviso that you stay together and search for the replica in a team of three. I believe that Miss Drew intends to keep her eye on you.'

Kathy and I were not enthused about running around the countryside under the eagle eye of Miss Drew until Mick told us that the prize for the winner of the Dymwich Hunt was a mammoth box of sweets. From that moment on Kathy and I were as intensely interested in finding the Dymwich Hunt scroll as old

Cromwell – sweets were in short supply and about to be rationed. A giant box of sweets would be worth hunting despite Vinegar Drew.

We asked friends in the village about the Dymwich Hunt and learned the evening before the fete Miss Drew and four girl guides hide a replica scroll at the end of one of a dozen trails that they had blazed using stones, sticks, tied grasses and chalk marks on trees and boulders. Every trail started on the Lesser Dymwich green but only one ended at the replica scroll.

Kathy, Mick and I held a Council of War the afternoon before the fete. Miss Drew locked Kathy and me in the tiny sewing room every evening – she even locked our small window so by default Mick won the job to shadow Vinegar and her guides when they laid the trails and hid the replica scroll. At the end of each false trail was a consolation prize of a book voucher.

I think Mick looked forward to trailing Vinegar and her girl guides in the dark, a short night's sleep was of little concern to a London Blitz boy.

Fete Saturday dawned warm and sunny. When Kathy and I walked to the village a stage draped with patriotic bunting had already been raised in the shade of the oak tree on the green and the villagers were decorating stalls and tents with red, white and blue flags…every living creature that walked on two legs or four wore patriotic red, white and blue colours.

We had arranged to rendezvous with Mick behind the big marquee and that's where we found him impatiently waiting. Mick had a tendency to show-off but he went over the top that day. His twilight mission had been a grand success. He had ignored the three guides who laid the false trails and stayed with Miss Drew and the guide who carried the replica scroll.

'Bet neither of you can guess where they hid the scroll.' Mick grinned at us.

'Can you guess where I'm going to kick you if you keep waffling?' I snarled.

'Me too,' Kathy actually drew back her foot.

'Gosh, being evacuated has turned you two into a couple of grumpy grannies – you're no fun at all. I should be your shining knight after last night.'

'You ain't living with Vinegar Drew,' Kathy pointed out.

'I can't argue with you on that point,' Mick reasonably conceded.

'So did you get the replica scroll?' I urged, 'I'm keen to taste a lemon drop.'

Mick tapped a bulge in his shirt with a wicked grin. 'Vinegar and the guide holding the replica scroll marked a trail that twisted for about a mile through the woods nearby and ended back here at the starting point...that old oak was a piece of cake to climb.'

'You've become an utterly brilliant bloke, Mick.' Kathy enthused in rare praise.

I warned, 'I agree with Kathy, it was a jolly good show Mick but Vinegar will be watching which way we run at the start of the Hunt so that she can follow us.'

'I've fixed that,' Mick grinned. 'Simon ain't eligible to compete in the Hunt and for a few sweets out of our prize he agreed to cause a diversion and distract Vinegar when we nick off.'

'The clean country air is doing wonders for your brains Mick Doherty,' Kathy beamed.

I had to agree that bribing Simon to distract Vinegar was smart, 'Do you reckon that he would be willing to hang about the green at the end of the Hunt in case we need Vinegar to look the other way when one of us pretends to find the scroll in the oak tree?'

'I've fixed that. Simon's sister was happy to play the game too...Vinegar is even meaner to the gypsies than she is to evacuees from London.'

Reverend Molland and Vinegar Drew were on the stage with the local squire who adjusted the microphone in preparation to starting the Hunt and I was resigned to a long boring speech but in spite of being a direct descendant of the Royalist squire who lost his head our squire kept his speech mercifully short. A groan went through the crowd when the squire passed the microphone to Reverend Molland who proceeded to give his audience a kindly meandering talk filled with obscure references to cricket.

Vinegar Drew constantly interrupted Reverend Molland's speech with stern cautions about trespass and littering and a grim warning that competitors who were not back on the green by the appointed end of the Hunt would forfeit any consolation book vouchers they may have collected along the way.

The replica scroll was dangling heavily in the right leg of my knickers when Reverend Molland finally wound up his long-winded speech and wished "Good hunting" to the large pack of impatient hunters who were fidgeting in front of the stage. I saw Vinegar Drew frown when she spotted us at the back of the crowd.

The squire reclaimed the microphone and fired a starter's pistol in the air and shrieking children hared off in every direction and Vinegar Drew's beady eyes were fixed on the three of us. She left the stage and was hurrying in our direction when her path was blocked by two gypsy boys having a noisy wrestling match. Simon and a pretty dark girl wearing a colourful headscarf and lots of beads and bangles were pretending to be trying to part the boys.

Kathy, Mick and I slipped away without a backward glance and ran down the lane we had chosen earlier. We crawled through a leafy hedge and scuttled like mice through the field of ripening golden corn that was on the other side of the hedge.

At the opposite side of the corn field was a dense hedge that lined the narrow dirt lane leading to the village of Dymwich Meadows about a mile away. Lesser Dymwich village was soon a mile behind us.

Our plan was wicked and simple. We planned to hide in the small wild wood outside the village of Dymwich Meadows where Simon had shown Mick the badger set and wait until an appropriate length of time had passed when we could leave the small wild wood and return to Lesser Dymwich where we would 'find' the replica scroll in the oak tree on the green so that we could claim the fabulous prize of a mammoth box of sweets.

Kathy and Mick had agreed that I should be the one to climb the oak-tree and pretend to find the scroll. Kathy dreamily murmured that she could smell chocolate frogs, anticipation of lemon drops caused my mouth to water and sweet-toothed Mick simply drooled with his imagination in overdrive in a world of confectionary.

We walked beside the dense hedge that lined the other side of the cornfield until we were fairly sure that we were opposite the badger wood. We pushed through the hedge and were shocked to find ourselves standing in front of the Green Man Inn on the far side of Dymwich Meadows village and four old men were sitting on a long rustic bench against the wall of the inn drinking ale – we had walked too far along the cornfield hedge.

The ale drinkers eyed our abrupt appearance through the hedge with interest and put down their tankards. We turned to run but retreat was halted by a loud voice with a disconcerting ring of authority.

'Where the Dickens did you youngsters spring from? Come here and give your names.'

We turned and faced a tall elderly man with a bushy white beard who had been sitting on the end of the bench. Kathy was our enchanting tiny golden haired angel and the kids from the buildings think fast. Mick's elbow ground into her ribs as I trod heavily on her foot. When we fronted up to Bushy Beard real tears glistened in Kathy's large innocent sky-blue eyes and a teardrop was slowly creeping down her creamy cheek. Her limp was genuine too.

'I'll get you both – later,' Kathy gritted quietly before she broke into loud wailing.

'Please Guv, we're lorst,' Mick rubbed Kathy's back as he whined at Bushy Beard, 'we've slogged for blooming miles but we can't find our bleeding village.'

I gave a long loud sniff as if I was about to join Kathy in her noisy misery.

'That's quite enough caterwauling from you girls.' Bushy Beard turned to Mick, 'are you and your two friends competing in the Dymwich Hunt?'

Mick was scandalised, 'no bleeding fear, Guv! We wouldn't chase a poor little fox with horses and then let a pack of savage dogs rip the poor little sod to bits.'

Kathy and I added our horrified disclaimers to Mick's righteous outrage at being thought a willing participant in the country blood-sport.

'The Major don't mean that kind of hunt dear,' said a plump lady who had appeared in the doorway of the inn. 'The poor mites must be evacuees from the London bombs.'

'This is Dymwich Meadows, which village did they billet you in?' Bushy Beard asked.

'It's called Dymwich something or other too.' I helpfully offered.

'Would that be Upper Dymwich, Lesser Dymwich, Dymwich Ponds, Dymwich Under The Hill or maybe it was Lower Dymwich?' The kindly lady asked.

Three pairs of worried and guileless eyes gazed blankly back at her.

Bushy Beard took control of the stressful situation. 'Come now, three lemonades and three bags of crisps, if you please Mrs Baker and no more interrogation. These brave soldiers must sit down and rest. The way back to their village may come to them when they have rested.'

Bushy Beard's prophecy came true after another round of lemonade and cries of the Hunt pack in the distance. We thanked our new friends effusively and ran down the dirt lane. The Green Man Inn and Bushy Beard were well out of view when we broke through the hedge and made a bee-line back to Lesser Dymwich.

There was no sign of Vinegar Drew in the curious crowd that stood with Mick and Kathy and watched me climb the oak tree and disappear in the leafy branches. The crowd burst into wild applause when I re-appeared waving the replica scroll victoriously over my head and the Reverend Molland was tickled pink that his 'London laddie' had led the winning team.

The noisy clapping and whistling brought Vinegar Drew and the pretty gypsy girl out of the fortune-teller tent. Vinegar was furious, flummoxed and flustered all at the same time when I handed the replica scroll to her with a polite smile. She gave me her basilisk glare and muttered so that only I heard, 'I swear that I will find out how you awful grubs did this if it takes the duration of the war.'

Prizes were to be presented to winners of the various raffles and competitions at the close of the fete and waiting with patience was hard but our glorious moment finally arrived and the squire called our names over the public address system and asked us to go up on the stage. We scarcely glanced at the local dignitaries seated in a line on the stage, our eyes were magnetised by a gigantic box in the hands of the beaming vicar. It was as if all the joys of a Christmas that we had known before the shortages of war had been wrapped in parachute silk and decorated with streamers of anti-radar foil and it was all ours – less the modest payments to Simon and his sister.

My taste buds were singing when Kathy shoved Mick and he stumbled forward with hands outstretched to accept our sweet reward but the smiling Reverend Molland turned and handed our treasure to someone standing directly behind him.

'Let us give a big hand to Major Handley-Carr who has graciously consented to present the victors of this year's Dymwich Hunt with their richly deserved prize.'

The crowd clapped and Mick's grey eyes widened with shock when he looked up into the arctic-blue glare of Bushy Beard's eyes.

Mick has never been at a complete loss for words and I believe he succinctly summed up the feelings of me and Kathy with his microphone amplified groan of, 'oh bugger!'

7

1941
the witch in Sumner Road Passage

During the Second World War thousands of men, women and children escaped occupied Europe and fled across the Channel to seek sanctuary in the British Isles. Enemy agents were known to be among the asylum seekers but some overly imaginative Britons envisioned more bizarre perils than mere spies among the refugees. Stories about Adolf Hitler's belief in the occult had provided rich fodder for cartoonists and comedians for years and the rumour swept through Sumner Road School that a Nazi witch lived in one of the six terraced houses in the short passage that runs beside the school and connects Peckham High Street with the top end of Sumner Road.

The rumour of the witch spawned many highly coloured tales and Mick told us some scary stories that his Gran had told to him but when we visited Paddy in his new lodgings in Waite Street and we told him about the witch he had shaken his head and he said, with a sad smile, 'witches belong in fairy tales. That poor old lady in the Sumner Road Passage has probably fled from the killing madness that has gripped the Continent.'

Our interest in the witch faded three weeks before Christmas when snow fell non-stop for a week and the snow was knee deep before it stopped falling and Mick invited Kathy and me to build a giant snowman with him when he came home from Sunday mass.

When the Doherty family came home from church that cold snowy Sunday Kathy and I were waiting outside the door of their flat dressed in our oldest and warmest clothes. Maureen gave us mugs of hot cocoa to drink and a slice of toast to eat while Mick changed out of his 'Sunday Mass' clothes and gobbled a hasty breakfast.

Building a giant snowman requires a lot of fresh snow and snow on the pavements and the road had changed to dirty icy slush. We finally opted to build our snowman in the padlocked school playground where lack of foot traffic on Sundays guaranteed an abundance of pristine snow. We climbed over the chained wrought iron gate in the iron railing fence that fronted Sumner Road and stood in thigh deep sparkling clean snow but we were not alone.

'Hey Arthur, look at who's come to play – it's Mickey Doherty and his girlfriends.'

Big Frankie Cobb and his snotty-nosed younger brother Arthur were also trespassing on the school grounds but they weren't building a snowman, they were putting the finishing touches to an ice-slide in front of the teachers' entrance. The next snowfall would camouflage their dangerous booby-trap.

Kathy groaned, 'It's the flaming Cobb yobbos.'

Mick yelled, 'wotcher Frankie.'

'Don't encourage them,' Kathy and I hissed together.

Mick grinned at us, 'the Cobb boys won't scram anytime soon so why don't we use their muscle to help build our giant snowman and beat the next snowfall?'

Normally we would spurn the Cobb's company but Mick had a point, the dull grey sky appeared close enough to touch; a sure sign that another heavy fall of snow was imminent. I sighed and when I nodded Kathy groaned her reluctant agreement.

'Frankie how about you and young Arthur build a giant snowman with us?' Mick asked.

Frankie was visibly taken aback by the totally unexpected invitation. He looked a puzzled query at his brother and when Arthur happily nodded Frankie shrugged his meaty shoulders.

'Okay, we're in.'

His runny-nosed sibling sniffed long and wetly, 'yeah – we're in.'

Despite Kathy's constant exhortations for Arthur to stop work and blow his nose we beat the next snowfall and created a giant lopsided snow sentry inside the school gate that would surprise the teachers and delight the students when they arrived in the morning.

The frigid air had numbed our fingers and toes and Arthur's eternally dripping nose had turned an unpleasant mashed strawberry red when Kathy, Mick and I decided to go home to my flat and roast chestnuts on the open fire. Frankie didn't want the rare social interaction to end. 'Don't go yet, Mickey. Stay wiv me and Arthur and we'll snowball the witch's house.'

Kathy answered for the three of us with a coldly polite, 'no thank you, Frankie Cobb.'

'I wasn't talkin' to you Blondie,' said Frankie.

'Nah...me big brother don't talk with twitty bimbos,' Arthur sniffed at Kathy.

Kathy frowned and said in a dangerously quiet voice, 'come over here Snotty-Nose, and call me a twitty bimbo.'

'Twitty bimbo, twitty bimbo,' squeaked foolish young Arthur from a safe distance.

What diminutive Kathy lacked in size she more than made up for in fighting ability and she had an explosive temper. Mick and I watched with great interest when Frankie and Arthur ran towards the high brick wall at the end of the playground and Kathy took off after them.

Mick and I didn't join in the chase, we were laughing too much at Kathy's impotent fury. Snow that was knee high on me was hip high on Kathy and long before she could close the gap the Cobb brothers made use of the school dustbins to clamber over the high brick wall and drop down into the passage that connected Sumner Road to Peckham High Street.

Kathy stood on top of a dustbin unable to climb any higher. When I reached the top of the wall I leaned down, grasped her outstretched arm and hauled her up to sit by my side. I called down to Mick, 'shake a leg, Mick or are you waiting for Hitler to surrender?'

Mick remained in the playground. 'I ain't mixing it with the old witch in the passage.'

'But you agreed with Paddy when he said that the witch stories were a load of codswallop made up to scare us kids and stop us taking a short cut through the passage when it's dark.'

Mick shook his head, 'get off the wall before she looks out of the window of number four and puts the bleedin' evil eye on the pair of you.' Mick sounded absolutely serious.

I had believed Mick to be immune from fear but there was no mistaking the dread in his in his voice as he implored us to join him in the safety of the playground. Mick had been our fearless protective brother for as long as Kathy and I could remember. Kathy could not accept a frightened Mick and she laughed, 'stop trying to pull our legs.'

'I ain't kidding – please come down Kathy.' Mick pleaded, 'me Gran says she's a witch and you know me Gran ain't never wrong about that black magic stuff.'

Kathy and I stared stonily at the male component of our trio until male pride felt the prick of feminine contempt and Mick slowly climbed the wall and sat between us; his face paled beneath his freckles when his eyes gravitated to the lace covered window of number four.

Frankie and Arthur hooted with laughter as they plunged around in the deep snow in the passage shouting a rude rhyme about a witch's cat and throwing big snowballs at the window of number four.

Kathy poked my ribs to get my attention. She pointed to a familiar red bicycle chained to the downpipe against the wall of number one. I couldn't put a label on what suddenly made me so uncomfortable. I was tempted to drop down into the school playground and run home. I knew that Kathy and Mick would follow me without question. The red bicycle belonged to Dr Cohen and all three of our families were registered at his surgery.

With no hope of a Cobb compliance I shouted, 'go home Frankie – leave the poor old lady alone or she might turn you and Arthur into two maggoty turnip heads.'

Frankie blew a raspberry in my direction and gave me the finger. 'Shut up, Four-Eyes.'

Arthur thumbed his runny strawberry nose and yelled, 'yeah – shut your gob, bossy cow. My big brother ain't scared of the witch or you.'

The social niceties dispensed with the Cobb brothers resumed their assault on the innocent facade of number four until Arthur hurled a solid ice-ball at the lace-covered window. The frosty air intensified the loud crack that followed the well-aimed ice missile and time stood still for long seconds, then the door of number four opened wide and an old woman rushed out into the snow with a furled umbrella raised high in her clenched fist. She was scary and full of threat when she ran at Frankie and Arthur Cobb waving her umbrella as she screamed strange foreign words that sounded like a terrible black magic curse would sound.

The Cobb brothers fled and who could blame them? With her straggly grey hair and her long black skirt and tasselled black wool shawl, the old woman who ran out of number four brandishing an umbrella came straight out of the Gingerbread House in Hansel and Gretel.

The dramatic pursuit ended when Fate intervened and the old lady's booted foot came down on a snow covered ice-slide and she sprawled on her back in the snow as her black stockinged legs helplessly kicked air and displayed long legged old-fashioned lace trimmed bloomers. Frankie and Arthur stopped running and returned to gloat

Frankie and Arthur scooped up big handfuls of dirty ice-slush and advanced upon their helpless prey who was trying to stand on the ice-slide. I signalled Mick and Kathy to slip away when Frankie shouted, 'go back to where you came from...we don't want you here.'

Frankie had labelled my uncomfortable feeling...

it was called shame. I dropped into the passage and snatched up the old lady's brolly from the snow and charged Frankie but I didn't go into battle alone – Mick ran beside me yelling his blood-curdling battle-cries.

Mick feared nothing which called for his handy fists. We were on the heels of the Cobb brothers as we neared the Co-op on Peckham High Street when Mick grabbed my arm and roughly jerked me to a standstill.

'Kathy! We've left her alone with the bleedin' witch – we've got to save her.'

Ignoring my exasperated protest that Kathy was safely perched on the top of a ten foot high wall Mick whirled about and raced back along Peckham High Street. I followed at a sedate trot but I still had a stitch in my side when I rounded the bend of the passage and saw Kathy sitting up in the snow with the old woman bending over her.

Then I saw what was probably one of the bravest and most certainly was one of the silliest acts of Mick's life, and there were plenty of those, Mick threw himself on top of Kathy and knocked her flat into the snow as he yelled at the startled old lady, 'Don't you dare try to put a spell on Kathy!'

Kathy struggled out from under Mick's protective bulk and her cornflower blue eyes blazed up at her would-be champion as she gritted, 'get off of me you big lunk! It was you who knocked me off the blinking wall – you great daft nit.'

Suddenly Dr Cohen was among us and scarlet with confusion, Mick scrambled off Kathy. Dr Cohen lifted her up on to her feet and brushed damp snow from her coat. He scolded me and Mick while he attached the shoulder cord of Kathy's gasmask box that had come adrift.

'I credited you two with more sense. The school wall is at least ten foot high and that's far too high for little Kathy to...' our doctor was silenced by the old lady's loud gasp.

'Is something wrong Mrs Goldstein?'

She was staring at Kathy as she rattled off a stream of quick foreign words and Dr Cohen was smiling when he replied in the same quick foreign language.

''ere! What did she say? What did you say?' suspicious Mick demanded for all of us.

'Mrs Goldstein said that Kathy hit the ground heavily when you pushed her off the wall.'

'I didn't push Kathy off the wall – you tell the old witch she's a liar.' Mick fumed.

'I've just explained to Mrs Goldstein that you would never deliberately hurt Kathy – but if you call this nice lady a witch again I will box your ears very hard Michael Doherty.'

Dr Cohen peered at a tiny red graze on Kathy's forehead, 'hmm, that injury warrants a closer examination but we'll turn into ice-sculptures if we stand here in this arctic blizzard for much longer.'

Snow was falling in a soft white curtain; not an arctic blizzard. Gran Doherty, our expert on Faerie and the occult, would say that Mother Carey was plucking her chickens. I became aware of the doctor's soft brown eyes studying me and alarm bells began ringing warnings of adult duplicity. I signalled retreat to Mick and Kathy but I was outflanked by the doctor when he stepped between me and Kathy and said briskly, 'let's get Kathy into Mrs Goldstein's warm parlour. Mrs Goldstein has offered to make us hot cocoa drinks.'

Mick's voice became shrill as he fumbled with the

buttons on his bomber jacket, 'Tell her thanks but no thanks. We ain't going into her parlour because we're going to Nell's flat to roast chestnuts – my coat will keep Kathy warm.'

I chipped in, 'my Dad will be so worried if I stayed out late in an arctic blizzard.'

Dr Cohen stared at me, 'I understand what you and Mick are saying Nell but if you can't accept Mrs Goldstein's invitation then I'll have to examine Kathy in her flat this evening. Of course that means I'll have to charge Mrs Henson for a home visit and when I complete the Ministry of Health forms I'll have to mention that Mick caused Kathy's accident.' He sighed, 'that's a lot of irritating paper-work I wouldn't have to do for a quick consultation in kind old Mrs Goldstein's warm parlour.'

I was flabbergasted. Blackmail! I'd always regarded our doctor as a good bloke until this day of revelations but worse was to come. Kathy and Mrs Goldstein smiled at each other and without so much as a fleeting glance at Mick or me they walked together to the open door of number four with Kathy's supportive hand under the old woman's elbow.

Dr Cohen raised his eyebrows at Mick and me.

'Well? Are you two rascals coming inside to join Kathy and me in a mug of hot cocoa with Mrs Goldstein in her warm parlour?'

Abandoning Kathy to the unknown dangers lurking inside number four was unthinkable but Mick still whimpered when I said breezily, 'we don't mind if we do – but we won't be staying long.'

Mick's unwilling feet dragged close behind me when I swaggered inside number four and as Mick stepped through the front-door he made the sign of the cross. Dr Cohen shepherded Mick and me into Mrs Goldstein's parlour where a cheerful fire was blazing hotly in a black leaded fireplace. Mrs Goldstein wasn't in the over furnished room but Kathy looked at home in a big stuffed armchair in front of the crackling fire.

The parlour was so heated I had to de-mist my glasses with my hanky so that I could see.

I ignored a sofa heaped with cushions that faced the fire and remained standing beside a lace draped table in the middle of the room. Mick was perched on the edge of a straight-backed chair beside the door – Mick was ready bolt the second a black cat or any other arcane sign put in an appearance.

Always an advocate of attack being the best strategy in a fight, especially an unequal fight, I faced up to the doctor. 'We reckon you should tell us what your game is, Dr Cohen.'

Instead of chipping me for cheek he nodded, 'That's fair enough Nell. When I watched you and Mick run off the Cobb brothers a few minutes ago I realised you were the youngsters I needed for a special job.'

'What kind of special job?' Mick and I chanted together.

He eyed us thoughtfully. 'I'm looking for friends for Mrs Goldstein, good friends who'll visit her regularly, run the odd errand and generally keep an eye on her so that hooligans such as the Cobb brothers don't bother her.'

His raised hand silenced our shocked chorus of refusal.

'Hear me out please. Mrs Goldstein is a lonely old lady. She has lived in this house for ten months yet not one of her neighbours has bothered to call in and see that she is okay after a heavy air-raid. Nobody has spoken to her in a shopping queue at the Co-op.'

'She dresses too weird for anyone to talk to her in the shops.' I muttered.

He shook his head and looked sad, 'it's true that Mrs Goldstein wears long dark skirts and black stockings and she doesn't talk like a Peckham lady. But how will she learn to fit into the neighbourhood if none of the neighbours will talk to her?"

'They've enough trouble with Hitler – they don't need witch trouble too.' Mick growled.

'Thanks to those silly witch stories you are the first young people to enter this house yet Mrs Goldstein has been a teacher all her life and loves children.'

I went on the attack – as I always did when confronted with a disconcerting truth, 'Who invited her to come here? She should go back to where she…'

I cringed into silence at the echo of Frankie Cobb and Dr Cohen didn't let me off his hook, 'I suspect that you and Mick felt ashamed when the Cobbs behaved badly to such a nice lady and that was why you stopped and chased the bullies.'

Kathy quietly asked, 'why has Mrs Goldstein come to live in England?'

'Mrs Goldstein is Jewish; do you know what is happening on the Continent at this very minute to people who are impaired physically or mentally, or were born with gypsy or Jewish blood in their veins?'

We were children of war and knew far too much of war's cruel insanity. We answered him with silent slow nods and lowered heads, only Kathy met Dr Cohen's eyes.

'Do you want to hear some of Mrs Goldstein's story before she comes in with our cocoa?'

'Yes, please.' Kathy whispered.

Mick and I remained silent. I sensed that Mick desperately wanted to be outside in the cold snow with a problem that he could handle – such as a punch-up with the Cobb boys.

Dr Cohen perched on the arm of Kathy's chair and started telling us the old woman's story. I tried to not listen but his voice was relentless.

'One moonless night last winter French resistance fighters smuggled a group of refugees across the Channel in a fishing trawler. Mrs Goldstein and her grand-daughter Katrina were among the desperate people crowded into the fish stinking blackness of the trawler's hold. The fishing-boat was two miles off Ramsgate when it was attacked and sunk by a patrolling Stuka dive-bomber. The survivors could only tread water and pray.'

Dr Cohen was aware that he was talking to veterans of war from the skies and he didn't go into details. He didn't have to explain to us that the Stuka pilot would have been strafing the survivors in the ocean with deadly machine gun fire.

I stared into the hot fire and studied the burning coals – I couldn't see any shapes that were remotely witch-like and I heard Kathy's whisper, 'how did Mrs Goldstein escape?'

'Spitfires eventually came from Biggin Hill and chased the Stuka dive-bomber away but when the rescue boats arrived from Ramsgate little Katrina was not among the survivors and Mrs Goldstein had no living family left anywhere in the world.'

I continued staring into the fire's glowing embers. To terrify people being attacked on the ground the Stuka dive bomber was fitted with a siren that screamed whenever the plane went into a steep dive and the refugees bobbing in the sea would have heard that awful screaming and the deadly chatter of guns as the Stuka dived on them like a hawk striking rabbits frozen with fear. The boat people would have suffered terribly in the freezing water, the Channel in wintertime is icy and cruel.

Kathy's big blue eyes were bright with tears when she whispered to me, 'I wouldn't mind keeping an eye on the old girl – I sort of like her.'

The doctor heard Kathy and smiled, he stabbed his forefinger at Mick and me. 'I heard a story that old Mr Kelly who used to live in Stanton Street beside the canal and now resides in a Waite Street boarding house, regards you three scallywags as his grandchildren and that you treat him as you would treat your own grandfather.'

We each gave a wary nod but Mick and I didn't like where the conversation was going.

Mick had a worried scowl on his freckled face when he asked, 'what does our looking out for old Paddy Kelly have to do with anything?'

'Well I was just wondering if Kathy would like to have a grandmother to visit as well as a grandfather.' He winked at Kathy who winked back at him with a shy smile.

I knew that Mick would have related to the doctor's story of the Stuka bomber's attack on the refugees but a fearsome shadow of dark magic still hovered over his ginger curls and as Mick always did when he became confused, he appealed to me and he whispered in my ear,

'Nell, the old girl's put a bleedin' spell on the Doc

and Kathy – you say the word and I'll grab Kathy and we'll scarper before she comes in with the cocoa.'

I stared into the glowing coals in the polished hearth and I saw Kathy's cold empty flat. Like me, Kathy carried her front door key on a string around her neck but there similarity in our lives ended. While we were building the giant snowman Kathy told me that her mother was sleeping over at the club that night and Kathy was cooking a dried egg omelette for her lonely dinner. Dr Cohen was right, Kathy did need a grandmother. I looked into his watchful brown eyes when I shrugged, 'perhaps we'll have a go at keeping an eye on Mrs Goldstein.'

Before Mick could protest Mrs Goldstein bustled into the room carrying a heavy wooden tray and chattering in her funny English. She placed the tray on the lace-covered table beside me and fragrant chocolate steam rose from five large china mugs. The mouth-watering scent filled the room but the tray held an even greater delight – a china platter heaped high with thick slices of rich fruit cake. In those bleak days of food rationing fruit cake was a luxury we only knew from coloured photos in cook-books. Both disbelief and utter bliss was on Mick's face as he gazed at the hill of luscious fruity slices and with a moan of pleasure he capitulated and in an instant the wicked witch was transformed into a fairy godmother. In Mick's world a nasty witch could never conjure such a heavenly treat – I always suspected that Mick would sup with the Devil himself if Old Nick served the right grub.

The big china platter was bare when we put on our coats to go home, we didn't leave a crumb. We each carried a generous slice of fruit cake wrapped in a sheet of writing paper and I looked forward to surprising my sweet toothed Dad. Mrs Goldstein told us that the luscious fruit cake had been in a Refugee Care package that came all the way from Australia and that she had been saving it for a special occasion and we were that special occasion.

Kathy kissed Mrs Goldstein's wrinkled cheek when we said goodbye and Granny Gold, as we later came to call her, dabbed her eyes with a corner of her long black shawl.

We shivered with cold in the deep snow of the passage while we waited for Dr Cohen to unchain his bicycle and give us a few parting words of adult wisdom.

'I am so proud of the three of you – you learned a valuable lesson about communication today. I believe that our leaders could end this terrible war if they would only sit down and communicate instead of firing bullets and dropping bombs on people.'

We solemnly agreed with Dr Cohen and when we watched him pedal away we agreed among ourselves that despite being tricky he really wasn't a bad bloke for a grown-up.

Fresh snow had fallen and covered the icy slush on the pavements while we were visiting Mrs Goldstein and we had to watch our footing when we trudged home along Sumner Road. Mick made Kathy wear his padded jacket over her thin coat and we talked over the unusual morning as we walked.

Mick asked Kathy and me, 'do either of you think that Doc was right about talking being a way to end the war?'

I shrugged, 'I find it hard to picture King George and Winnie having a natter with Adolf over mugs of hot cocoa and slices of fruit cake.'

Kathy said quietly, 'the trick to get them talking would have to be to knock the buggers off their high walls without breaking their blooming necks.'

I knew exactly what Kathy was trying to say in her gentle way.

For many months Granny Gold and Kathy Henson shared a lot of love and happiness.

8

1942
Paddy Kelly's choppers

During times of pressing financial need the pawnshop of yesteryear provided an essential banking service for families on low income. Often run as a family business from a dingy shop discreetly tucked away in a back street an old-time pawnshop could be found in every town. Three brass balls suspended over the front door denoted that the owner was a licensed money lender legally able to make financial loans. Regular customers called the pawnbroker 'uncle' and the local 'uncle' could calculate to a farthing the amount of money a regular customer would be able to repay. This was a vital skill in the days when anything was accepted from a regular customer as a token pledge for a small loan…even a set of dentures.

In the 1940s there was a small pawnshop on Peckham High Street next to the entrance of the passage that connects Peckham High Street with the top end of Sumner Road. The owner was Cecil C. White, at least that was the name printed in neat gilt letters underneath the three brass balls suspended over the front door. The owner was called 'Snow' by customers and old Paddy Kelly was one of Snow's regular customers. Second-hand treasure and junk that was crammed onto the dusty shelves in Snow's shop was unredeemed collateral that was traded at a small profit.

Today's pawnbroker makes legal financial loans under the franchise umbrella of a large finance company and trades quality second-hand goods in a modern shop in an upmarket section of town.

I was in the flat getting ready for school when I glanced out of the front-room window and saw Paddy in the street below standing on the pub corner and I thought that Paddy must have stopped on the corner for a breather and perhaps the chance to say hello to us on our way to school...shops in Peckham High Street were a long walk from Waite Street.

By the time I left the flat and went downstairs Paddy had gone and Kathy and Mick were standing on the corner. I asked them, 'did you see Paddy? He was here just minutes ago.'

Mick showed me three half-crowns wrapped in a pawnshop ticket, 'Paddy gave me these. He's gone home to have a kip after walking all the way from Waite Street.'

'What shopping does he want from the Co-op?'

'Nothing from the co'op. The poor old sod ain't 'ad a decent bite to eat since he hocked his choppers with Snow a week ago. He got his pension yesterday but Snow isn't opening until eleven this morning. When I get a chance I'm nicking out of school in the lunch break to get Paddy's choppers out of hock for him.'

Kathy raised her eyebrows at me, 'Mick thinks he will impress Sally Taylor if he shows off Paddy's awful old teeth at school. Maureen warned him that she will strangle him and us if he puts so much as a toe out of line after our evacuation cock-up in Lesser Dymwich.'

Mick scowled at Kathy, 'Give over Kath, I'll be saving old Paddy from starvation.'

Kathy was on a roll, 'suppose you get caught nicking out at lunchtime? It will be your fault if I'm evacuated to some foreign land because you broke the strictest rule in the school. My mother is just itching for an excuse to ship me off to Australia or Canada.'

'I reckon Gloria will understand if she knows that I broke the school rule for Paddy.'

Mick and Kathy continued to bicker until we reached the school gate. Until the home bell rings students were not permitted to leave the school grounds after morning assembly without written sanction and Mick planned to grab the first opportune moment during lunch break to scale the high wall at the side of the school playground, drop into Granny Gold's passage and redeem Paddy's ugly old dentures from the hock-shop in Peckham High Street. Kathy and I gave Mick our support – as we always did. The streets were littered with bomb debris after the night's air-raids and we had no trouble convincing our more observant class-mates that Mick had climbed over the wall to retrieve a body part that he had spotted in the passage on his way to school...we were possibly led astray by Boris Karloff who despondently lumbered across the screen of the Odeon cinema all week as Frankenstein's unhappy monster.

When stubborn Mick came back over the wall he was holding a small newspaper wrapped

Sally Taylor was at the forefront of the small but intensely interested audience that Kathy and I mustered in the girl's cloakroom. The girls crowded around Mick as he slowly opened the small newspaper wrapped parcel and awed gasps escaped the onlookers when the set of large ugly yellowed teeth were finally revealed.

Mick acted a showman role well, 'come closer girls and take a good look at the amazing effect a bomb had on some poor old geezer's choppers – bumped them right out of his gob.'

When Kathy saw that Mick had Sally Taylor's rapt attention she snorted with impatience and flicked the end of his nose.

'False teeth can't be bumped out of someone's mouth. Tell us what else can these clever choppers can do, Romeo?'

'They can bite the noses of saucy blondes.' Mick closed the hideous teeth on Kathy's nose and she ran screaming out of the cloakroom with Mick in pursuit snapping the awful dentures in her flying blonde hair. There was a sound of bodies colliding in the corridor outside the girl's cloakroom. I squeezed into the crush of girls in the cloakroom doorway. Kathy, Mick and Mr Rolls were sitting on the floor of the corridor in what could have been a story-telling circle if all three of them hadn't looked so stunned. All these years later I still regret missing the actual moment of impact between Kathy, Mick and old Crusty Rolls. Going by the sheets of paper all over the floor Mr Rolls had been carrying a stack of carefully cut up butcher's paper...writing paper was a luxury in wartime. Mr Rolls was one of the patriotic teachers who came out of retirement to teach part-time in the war-created teacher shortage. A rumour that he was a hundred years old may have been true. He was toothless, short-sighted, deaf, and had an erratic memory. Girls that were in Crusty's classes were thankful that he taught for only two days of the week... he never hid his intense dislike of the female gender.

'I'm so sorry, Mr Rolls. Are you hurt?' Kathy was genuinely concerned.

Crusty peered into her worried face and snapped, 'of course I'm hurt, you stupid girl.' He turned to Mick, 'running isn't permitted inside the school and you should be aware of that ruling Michael Doherty. Did this stupid girl cause you to break the school rule?'

'She may have. I'll tell the silly cow off good and proper later Sir,'said Mick the Weasel in his humblest voice.

Crusty was appeased, 'I want to see one hundred lines, "I must not run inside the school" waiting for me in the staff-room from each of you when I come to teach school next Friday.'

'Yes Mr Rolls,' the guilty pair chanted happy in the knowledge that old Crusty will have forgotten the collision by next week.

Mick was helping the old teacher to his feet when Crusty saw the teeth in Mick's hand and he moved with surprising speed and plucked Paddy's ugly teeth from Mick's nerveless grasp while Mick was distracted by the clanging of the afternoon class bell.

'Good man Doherty! Well fielded old chap,' Crusty bellowed with enthusiasm.

We watched aghast as Crusty carefully wrapped the yellowed fangs in a large blue polka dot handkerchief and then pushed the polka dotted parcel into the top pocket of his jacket. Mick's freckled face flushed when he heard Sally Taylor and her chums sniggering as they made good their escape around our comic tableau.

Crusty confided to Mick, 'always look after your teeth Michael. I paid good money for these dentures only two years ago but they're so uncomfortable now I can only wear them to eat. On the days I come to school I leave them in a container in the staffroom between meals. I've been measured for a new set of dentures but every time I ask if my new teeth are ready I'm told to be patient because there's a war on.'

He frowned and said in a puzzled voice, 'I don't understand. I had soup for lunch today because I was sure that I had left my teeth at home but it seems that they were in my mouth.'

Crusty beamed a gummy smile at Mick, 'thanks to your quick hands my boy there was no damage done and I'll be able to enjoy my dinner tonight.'

I stared in horror at a line of polka dots peeping from the breast pocket of Crusty Roll's jacket and wondered how poor Paddy would eat his dinner that night without his teeth.

Kathy became reckless and gave Crusty an angelic smile, 'please Sir – I'll take your teeth upstairs to the staff-room if you want to soak them in water this afternoon.'

His pale gooseberry eyes stared coldly at Kathy's pretty earnest face, 'get along to your classroom you silly girl.'

Kathy knew that she had wasted her angelic smile when old Crusty Rolls stalked off along the corridor muttering an anti-female mutter.

Mick's worried eyes turned to me, 'bleeding 'ell – what'll we do now, Nell?'

'Kathy and I will do nothing,' I hissed, 'you lost Paddy's choppers – you get 'em back.'

Mick went into panic mode. 'What the 'ell can I do? I've got science wiv the new bloke this afternoon and he never misses a bloody trick...help me Kathy.'

Kathy gave him a fierce ultimatum, 'you get Paddy's choppers back – or look out.' Kathy added in a menacing tone, 'and double look out if you ever call me a silly cow again.'

Two smouldering Amazons stalked away from one very nervous man-child.

There was scant equality between the sexes in the 1940s and the feminist inside me always surfaced on science afternoon when the genders were segregated at Sumner Road School and girls went downstairs to a purpose built kitchen in the basement and learned their preordained role in life in a class with the euphemistic name 'Domestic Science' while boys went upstairs to a specially equipped science room and did exciting stuff with Bunsen burners.

That afternoon classes were disrupted by two air-raids and the headmaster dismissed the school early after the All-Clear siren's second long howl. Mick was waiting with a big grin on his face to walk with Kathy and me to the school-gate.

'Why are you looking like the cat that ate the canary?' Kathy demanded suspiciously.

Still grinning Mick slapped his battered school satchel, 'chopper mission successfully accomplished. Paddy can eat whatever he fancies tonight.'

'How on Earth did you manage that?' Kathy and I chorused in disbelief.

Mick's grin grew wider, 'it was as easy as falling off a log. When the alert siren sounded I got the Hopkins twins to stage a punch-up on our way downstairs to the basement and while the new bloke was sorting the twins I nicked into the teachers' staffroom. Paddy's choppers were soaking in a glass jar of water with Crusty Rolls moniker on the lid.'

Kathy and I were very impressed by Mick's quick thinking and daring commando-style action and he basked in the glow of our admiration and dismissed our caution that Crusty was likely to re-think the puzzle of the teeth, 'nah, Crusty has a bad memory problem. When he sees the empty jar I bet he thinks that he had dreamed putting teeth into the jar and that he really did leave his choppers at home today.'

Kathy was doubtful, 'will he think that he was dreaming when we crashed in to him and he thanked you for catching the teeth he had been sure he left at home.'

Mick shook his head. 'His teeth are still at home. He'll think that he imagined us running into him in the corridor and I bet he hasn't said a word to the other teachers. I've heard that he's getting really embarrassed about imagining and forgetting things.'

Kathy sighed, 'poor old Crusty, he'll never work out what really happened today. I'm glad that he will find his teeth are waiting for him when he gets home.'

Kathy had an over-abundance of empathy – she even cried for Frankenstein's monster.

'Well if Crusty does smell a rat he'll guess that we three were in it up to our necks.' I had to whisper because Crusty was walking out of the school gate a few steps ahead of us.

Mick winked at me; Mick could be far too cocky at times. He ran and caught up with the old teacher outside the school gate.

'Ta, Ta, Mr Rolls – see you at school next week.'

'Goodbye Michael and thank you again for that magnificent catch. My teeth are safe now and I'm not taking them out of my pocket until I get them safely home.'

Then to our horror Crusty Rolls patted his jacket pocket. Mick was disconcerted for only a fleeting moment but he recovered fast. 'How could I catch your teeth sir? Didn't you say that you had left your teeth at home today, sir?'

'Of course you're making a joke.' A gummy smile came with the Crusty Rolls version of boy humour. He took a polka dot wrapped package from his top pocket, placed it inside his briefcase and Old Crusty Rolls walked away up Sumner Road taking Paddy's teeth beyond our reach forever.

Mick scowled at the set of even white teeth he took out of his satchel. 'The silly old sod didn't forget to bring his choppers from home this morning after all.'

'Can't you see that those teeth are too white and too normal for Paddy's teeth?' I asked.

'Nell's right they're nothing like Paddy's teeth.' Kathy unhelpfully agreed with me. 'Did you still have your his mind on Sally Taylor. After all it was your attempt to impress Miss Beautiful that caused you to lose Paddy's teeth in the first place.'

Mick glared at Kathy and me, 'I had to dodge getting sprung in the teachers' staffroom didn't I? And I didn't see either of you two bright sparks having a go at getting old Paddy's choppers back from enemy territory.'

'Shut it both of you and put your brains to work.' I firmly put a stop to their argument and set in motion a council of war on the long slow walk to Waite Street.

I tried to sound positive, 'we've forgotten that Paddy

is every bit as old as Crusty. I bet he only puts his teeth into his mouth to eat too. His eyes are not too good either, he has to use a magnifying glass to read. There's every chance that Paddy won't even notice that we brought back the wrong teeth to him.'

Mick was quick to agree with me, 'I think you're right Nell, there's a good chance that he won't spot the switch. It's not as if Paddy had his choppers specially made. He told me that he bought them second hand from Snow years ago.'

Sounding more optimistic Kathy contributed, 'Crusty might even get his new teeth sooner after he shows Paddy's awful yellow choppers to the dentist.'

A trio of prisoners marching to the guillotine could not have felt more despondent than we did on that long walk down Sumner Road to Waite Street in August sunshine bearing a wrong set of dentures to our dear old friend. We all wished that if a squad of German paratroopers planned to invade Peckham that they would get on with it and float down before we reached Waite Street but only small white clouds and of course the elephantine barrage balloons filled the pale autumn sky over our doomed heads.

Paddy's obvious pleasure at our arrival when he opened the door to Mick's knock made us feel too guilty to refuse his invitation to step inside for a brief visit and he did nothing to ease our tormented consciences when he offered us a bundle of old comics he'd rescued from a public paper salvage bin.

The moment we were dreading finally came as Kathy and I squabbled over an unread Beano. We froze when we heard Paddy ask, 'Mick boyo, was you having any trouble with me little errand to Snow?'

'Not a bit.' Mick slowly handed the newspaper wrapped teeth to Paddy. 'Snow gave me a tanner change for you.'

'Keep it for your trouble Mick.'

'No he can't!' Kathy and I exploded in unison and Paddy's shaggy eyebrows rose. His eyebrows were still elevated when he ran cold water over the bright white teeth at the sink. Three pairs of eyes watched mesmerised when he slipped the teeth into his mouth and Mick said hastily, 'the girls are right. We've all earned extra pocket money this week.'

We held our breaths when Paddy opened the tin with changing the guard at Buckingham Palace on the lid and selected a choice piece of broken biscuit. He slowly chewed and when he finally spoke he sounded curious, 'here's an odd thing, I bought these teeth from Snow many years ago and they've never properly fitted... until today.'

Three sets of young lungs expelled three gusts of held breath.

Paddy took another appreciative bite of biscuit before his bright blue eyes caught and held my terrified gaze, 'Nell, me clever colleen, do you think I should be asking Snow if he has made a mistake and given my bumpy old teeth to some poor stranger?'

I shook my head violently and my words tripped over themselves as I talked too fast. 'No don't do that! Snow has lots of choppers on his shelves that will never be redeemed. Owners have got bombed or bought new teeth or something…or anything. Perhaps Snow dropped and broke your old teeth. I bet they got nicked when Snow wasn't looking?'

The patent disgust on Kathy and Mick's faces told

me what they thought of my convoluted fabrication and Mick charged headlong into the breach, he was always a more convincing liar than Kathy or me.

'Maybe Snow thought that you deserved a better set of teeth. After all Paddy, you've been doing business wiv' Snow since forever.'

Paddy slowly nodded. 'That I have and mayhap you're right, but although I've always found Snow honest I've never known him to be guilty of a generous act.'

'Well wot I say is, if Snow didn't give you a better set of choppers out of the kindness of his 'eart then he's made a mistake and Snow's a proud bloke – he'd 'ate being caught out in a cock-up, it might be kinder if you kept shtum.' Mick's grey eyes were filled with sincerity.

'That was blarney logic at its' very best my brave boyo.' Paddy's bright blue eyes gravely studied each one of us in turn. 'Very well, 'tis settled then. I'll accept these beautifully fitting white teeth with gratitude and just a small touch of silent wonder.'

Our relief must been obvious it was so intense. Paddy held the open biscuit tin out to us. 'Here have some bits while there's some left. All those years living in Stanton Street at the side of the canal has sharpened the old nose and I smell rat.'

Kathy instantly dropped into a crouch and peered with apprehension into the shadowed corners of the pokey kitchen. Paddy chuckled and lifted her up on to her feet, 'don't be afraid my pretty one – there are only three of the scamps.'

Mick burst out laughing from sheer relief and when Paddy laughed along with him Kathy and I joined in — we hadn't pulled the wool over his wise old eyes but he would ask no more questions. He trusted and loved us as much as we trusted and loved him.

Before today's keeper of the family purse looks askance at the hard pressed mothers of years gone by who pawned family goods for a small cash loan perhaps they should quietly reflect on their use of today's credit card... a rose by any name?

9

1942
a penny for the guy

The traditional fireworks and bonfires of Guy Fawkes Night had been cancelled by louder fireworks and bigger fires of war but there was keen rivalry among kids from the buildings to create the Guy Fawkes that earned the most pennies and Kathy, Mick and I were determined to create the most lucrative Guy ever paraded in Rye Lane.

Mick scrounged enough clean straw from the local stables to make a solid body for a Guy that would fit in Mick's handcart. For his clothes we had a pair of torn trousers and a shirt that we salvaged from a bomb site and Maureen had washed and to finish off our guy's outfit my father gave up his jacket that was scorched in the stable fire and he added a truly horrible tie that an aunt had given him. Gran was so impressed by our straw man in his wheeled cart that she gave us two pennies to buy a papier-mâché mask from Woolworths in Rye Lane but best of all, Kathy donated Charlie's legendary hat.

Charlie was the milkman's much loved carthorse who had recently died of extreme old age. Kathy often fed

Charlie a carrot or an apple and the milkman had given her Charlie's famous hat as a memento of her friendship with the old horse. The straw sombrero had the invitation "KISS ME QUICK" printed in bold black letters on a wide red ribbon around the crown and Charlie's large hairy ears would poke up out of holes the milkman had cut out of the hat for that very purpose.

The milkman's wife bought the large brimmed sombrero in the Kursaal on a charabanc outing to Southend-On-Sea on a hot sunny day before the war and she thought the wide-brimmed hat would keep the sun out of Charlie's eyes on milk delivery rounds. The old carthorse had so loved his hat that he refused to put a hoof outside his stable without his fancy titfer.

It was the second week in October and we were still building our guy when the news ran like wildfire through Peckham that the popular back-street bookie Flash Fred was home on leave from the navy and he was accepting wagers on the weekend races.

Fash Fred had been a vision of sartorial elegance in working-class Peckham until the War Office insisted that he exchange his sharp suits for naval bell bottoms. No workman's cap hid the Brylcreem sheen of Flash Fred's slicked-back hair and his legs never bore the weight of a labourer's clodhoppers but the sharp dressing little bookie had a loyal following among the manual workers in the area

When a local family fell upon hard times the first helping hand to reach out to them was the well manicured hand of the jockey-sized Flash Fred. If the poor and vulnerable needed a champion in their corner then Flash Fred was always ready to do battle on their behalf.

The good-hearted dandy and his impossibly blonde lady lived in Melon Street, a narrow street off Peckham High Street that connects with the top end of Sumner Road via a short passage-way. Flash Fred observed the old-time gambler's superstition of throwing small luck away before the start of a big race and on significant days in the racing calendar Fred would walk through the estate playground throwing handfuls of small coins into the air and an army of children would scramble to pick up the scattered farthings, halfpennies and pennies and of course the kids from the buildings were among Flash Fred's staunchest supporters.

When Friday October 16th dawned all that we needed to complete our Mr Guy Fawkes was the mask that we were going to buy after school in the big Woolworths in Rye Lane with the two pennies Gran had given us. The mask had to match-up with Charlie's hat that hung in a string-bag underneath Kathy's coat in the girls' cloakroom all day on Friday. There was a strong smell of horse sweat in the girl's cloakroom when the home bell clanged.We knew that we wouldn't have much time to to choose our guy's mask. A mist that had crept in during the afternoon was thickening to fog.

When we crossed Peckham High Street we were puzzled by the unusual number of black caped policemen patrolling both sides of Rye Lane until we met Mick's brother Danny selling newspapers outside Boots Chemist and he explained the large police presence for us.

'The coppers jumped Flash Fred in the pub at the top of the Lane. He got away but he's trapped in the Lane with his bag of betting slips and money for tomorrow's races. I don't think the Flash can give the the rozzers the slip – the Old Bill's everywhere in the Lane.'

It was breaking the law to be a backstreet bookie but when you are eleven years old the heart tends to be the arbiter of right and wrong and in this instance our sympathies lay with the fox and we wished grand confusion on the hounds.

We knew that thanks to a fast thickening fog we had no time to chat with Danny before darkness would be upon us and we only had a small blue-papered torch to guide us safely back to the buildings in the black-out and not one of dared arrive home late.

My summertime curfew was negotiable but Dad insisted on me being inside our flat by four thirty in wintertime. When I demurred that he was being a tad strict Dad had reminded me that Mick, Kathy and I were still on probation for our misbehaviour as evacuees last year and we were in a similar curfew bind with Maureen.

Despite the curfews it took forty minutes of deliberation before we selected a comic Adolf Hitler mask that perfectly matched Charlie's hat and when we passed through the black-out curtains that draped Woolworth's doorway it was a minute after four thirty, the daylight was gone and the fog had thickened to a pea-souper. We had to trust that the dim blue light of my tiny pen-torch would lead us safely to our flats in the Sumner Road buildings where we knew we would all be in deep hot water.

Kathy clutched the string-bag with the precious hat and mask against her chest with one hand and gripped my coat belt with the other. Mick held the back of Kathy's coat and we prepared to start a dark walk home. The dense smog muffled the sounds of the shoppers who appeared and disappeared with startling rapidity through the thick blackout curtains cloaking Woolworth's doors. The shoppers emerging from the store instantly vanished into the dark dense smog.

We had taken no more than two steps into the dirty brown gloom when we were halted by a strange sound, 'Phsst!'

The strange sound came again, 'Phsst!'

Mick silently pointed to a large paper salvage bin waiting for collection in Woolworth's doorway. The salvage bin was filled to the brim with recyclable paper and cardboard. Mick touched a warning finger to his lips and leaned over the bin.

'Blimey! It's bleeding Flash Fred.'

Our benefactor's worried face rose slowly from a sea of paper and cardboard boxes. 'Wotcher Mick, 'allo, girlies – can you see any rozzers close by?'

Mick was first to find voice, 'no but they're all over the Lane – there's a bobby on watch outside Jones and Higgins and another one is standing on the opposite corner.'

Flash Fred cradled his fabled black race bag in his arms as if it were a new-born baby. 'Who would have dreamed the Old Bill would pounce on a Friday? How will I get home?'

We were far too street wise to suggest that he trust his race bag to us. Flash Fred would not voluntarily relinquish his precious black bag of betting slips to anyone.

Danny's voice came eerily through the fog, 'evening papers! Read the latest war news!'

I was struck by a sudden blindingly brilliant idea. I had a quick whispered conference with my two cohorts who nodded instant agreement. Mick spun around and disappeared into the thick brown smog.

‘Here! Where did young Mick run off to? Are you kids grassing me?’

I spoke with more confidence than I felt. ‘Of course not, we’re going to sneak you out of the Lane right under the Old Bill’s nose but you must do exactly what we tell you...if you don’t do exactly what we say, you’ll get us nicked too and then we’ll all go to prison.’

‘Don’t talk daft girlie – kids don’t get sent to prison,’ said Flash Fred.

Kathy scolded, ‘they might – there’s a war on in case you hadn’t noticed.’

I explained, ‘The coppers are a dead cert to check out this salvage bin so Mick’s gone to get your ride home.’

‘What’s the plan?’ he sounded like a drowning man clutching at three young straws.

‘Show him the rest of our plan Kathy.’

Kathy took Charlie’s hat and the Hitler mask from her string bag. ‘When Mick returns you’ll have to wear these.’

Flash Fred stared for a second at the comic mask and Charlie’s famous hat and with a loud groan of horrified disbelief he slowly sank under the loose papers.

Kathy and I waited several anxious minutes until Mick emerged from the smog pushing Danny’s wooden handcart sans newspapers before him. The empty handcart was draped with a large square of damp dirty canvas.

We coaxed and bullied Flash Fred into leaving the doubtful safety of the salvage bin. The sound of a fog-muffled police whistle aided our persuasion. Flash Fred was a small man but it was still a tight squeeze to cram him and his precious black bag into Danny’s handcart. Kathy and I suffered several attacks of nervous giggling before Flash Fred was eventually settled to our satisfaction – if not to his. When we covered him up to his neck with the grimy canvas he had an inkling of our plan and he was silent while Kathy fitted the Adolf mask over his face, it was when I pulled Charlie's hat firmly down over his slicked back oiled hair that he loudly protested.

‘'ere! Where the bleeding 'ell 'as this bloody hat been?'

'Shh! Remember the coppers,' we hissed in triplicate and he was silent when we set off down Rye Lane. The cart was awkward to steer on small skate wheels and we made slow progress down Rye Lane with Mick pushing the handcart while I helped to steer.

Kathy walked in front of us loudly calling, 'a penny for the Guy – please spare a penny for our Guy Fawkes.'

A soldier muffled up against the fog clipped the back of Mick's head and told us we were too early for Guy Fawkes but he gave us a ha'penny and an old lady gave us a farthing and told us to hurry home before we got caught out in a air-raid. Kathy had a penny, a halfpenny and three farthings in her beret by the time we reached the bottom of Rye Lane.

Patrolling policemen showed no interest in our Guy – except for the nice one on the corner of the High Street who gave us the penny because Adolf Hitler's face on a Guy Fawkes made him laugh.

When we reached the end of Rye Lane Mick whispered in our Guy's ear, 'a bumpy ride across the tram tracks is coming up – you're on the home stretch now Flash.'

We were easing the handcart off the pavement on to the road when a colossus in a black cape materialised from the smog and my heart raced. The giant was Sergeant Jack Brown who not only lived in Bude House he was a good friend of my father.

'Here! Here! What's all this about then?'

A 35 tram clanged a fog warning bell as it clattered slowly past three helpless rabbits transfixed by the killing stare of a giant stoat in a big black cape.

Kathy squeaked, 'penny for the Guy…if you please sir.'

The giant growled, 'It's far too late for you kids to be out in foggy weather. Especially you Nell Smith. Suppose Jerry pays us a call while you're so far from your shelter?'

'Our Guy has earned more than a penny so we're on our way home now Uncle Jack.'

He wagged a big finger at me, 'you'll find more than a pennyworth of trouble waiting for you when you get home Nellie. Now listen, if I see you three demons and Mr Fawkes safely across the High Street I want a solemn word from each one of you that you'll run home to the buildings with no more mucking about with Guy Fawkes.'

We nodded in unison and to our dismay Guy Fawkes got caught up in the moment and also nodded. Sergeant Brown chuckled, 'Herr Hitler is losing his bonnet – I'll fix him.'

Before any of us could speak a word a giant arm lifted and a police truncheon descended with a sickening thud and squashed Charlie's hat down to the red ribbon. I froze, Mick's lips moved with silent pleas to his favourite saint and Kathy burst into tears.

'There Adolf won't lose his fancy titfer now,' the giant smiled kindly down at Kathy who was sobbing, 'don't cry, dearie. I'm not really cross with you, I was young myself once and I loved banger night when I was a nipper.' He took over the propulsion of the handcart from Mick. 'Crikey! Did you stuff Adolf with bricks? He weighs a ton.'

The giant charged off into the fog pushing the handcart before him as if it was a battering ram and he was attacking a castle keep. Our Guy swayed wildly when the hand cart bumped over the tram tracks in the centre of Peckham High Street and we scurried in the giant's wake just thankful that Charlie's fancy titfer was now firmly jammed on the Guy's head. Safe on the opposite pavement we profusely thanked the large Sergeant for his help and repeated our promises to go straight home.

We waited on the pavement until Sergeant Brown vanished in the smog before we turned our attention to the ominously silent Guy. Mick's hand reached out to the hat and mask but Kathy's whisper that the hat might be all that was keeping Flash Fred's brains in their rightful place and Mick pushed the handcart on as fast as the small skate wheels would permit until we were standing outside Flash Fred's front door in Melon Street.

Mick gingerly removed the canvas draped around Fred's shoulders and we were relieved to hear small noises behind the mask. Sacrificing our financial investment of tuppence I snapped the mask's thin elastic on both sides and gently lifted Hitler's face off Flash Fred's face – I left Charlie's hat jammed down over his eyes.

Kathy hammered on Flash Fred's front door with the door's heavy iron knocker and Flash Fred's blonde lady threw open the door, 'Clear off you cheeky little sods…' her angry protest died on her bright red lips when she recognised the lower half of our Guy's face.

'Oh my gawd is that you Freddy my love...all boxed up in that little cart? I'll kill the little bleeders. What have they done to you my love?'

She unpacked Flash Fred with tender care and to our unspeakable relief he could stand up with her support. Charlie's sombrero still covered his eyes and he made piteous noises but he stood on his own two feet with his fabled black bag clutched close to his chest.

'What do you want me to do, Freddy my love?' cooed his anxious blonde lady.

Flash Fred seemed to have trouble speaking but the words finally came, 'git this 'at off my head and give the little. . .sods half-a-crown each.'

The hard wallop with a police truncheon had caused him to forget our names but we were brimming with joyous rapture. Two whole shillings and sixpence each – none of us had ever known such wealth and just in time for Christmas. It was more than fair recompense for the adult wrath that was waiting for each of us at home.

The blonde lady's thickly powdered nose wrinkled when she handed Charlie's hat to Kathy.

'Strewth! That hat stinks like an old carthorse!'

10

1942
Bagwash Billy

I was living in Queensland Australia in 1962 when I glanced through a woman's magazine and saw the photograph of a celebrity wedding in Sydney. A large man with a badly scarred face stood beside the happy bride and groom and his ugly face was beaming with pride and love. A caption beneath the wedding photograph said that the scar-faced giant was the brother of the lovely young bride and I was instantly transported back to my childhood in south east London during the Second World War and when I read the article that accompanied the photo I was filled with conflicting emotions.

The article claimed that the brother of the bride was a self-made multi-millionaire who had immigrated to Australia from the U.K. in the late 1940s. His hulking size and scarred face gave him an intimidating appearance but the magazine article described the brother of the bride as a kindly generous philanthropist lauded world-wide for his support and protection of disadvantaged children.

I knew the brother of the bride in 1942 when his name was Bagwash Billy and he was the resident bully at Sumner Road School – whenever he deigned to attend school. He wagged school so much that at thirteen going on fourteen years of age Bagwash Billy could barely read and write and he was so aggressive that people who cared were unable to help him.

Bagwash Billy spent his final year of formal education in a class of eleven year olds at the Sumner Road School...the same over-crowded class as Kathy, Mick and me. Billy was big for his age and so belligerent that the school's overworked teaching staff looked forward to his birthday in August when he would be fourteen and legally old enough to leave school.

Billy lived with his single mother and new-born baby sister in the basement of a house in Cator Street. The little family used to free-squat in a vacant run-down house in Lisford Street until the house was demolished to make way for the Sumner Road Housing Estate and Billy chose to believe that the eviction of his family from gratis housing gave him dispensation to bully the kids from the buildings and steal their possessions.

Bagwash Billy earned his nickname when he began a laundry delivery service. He charged four pennies to take a large bag of dirty clothes in his hand-cart to the Dutch Boy laundry in Peckham Hill Street before school in the morning and then he would deliver the heavy bag of damp clean washing smelling strongly of bleach back to the customer after school. Billy was illiterate in reading and writing but was strangely gifted with numbers and could do complex arithmetic in his head from an early age. He was also financially honest and could be trusted to pay a laundry bill and always bring the correct change back to the customer.

Within twelvemonths Bagwash Billy built up a thriving business. The housewives living on the upper balconies of the new Sumner Road Housing estate were especially appreciative of his reliable door to door laundry service and often added a small tip to his bill.

The staff at the Dutch-Boy bag-wash laundry also admired hard-working illiterate Billy and allowed him to identify his customer's bags with numbered tags but in June 1942 a new manager arrived at the Dutch-Boy laundry and he proved to be an inflexible new broom who insisted that Billy write invoices and receipts if he wanted to keep his delivery service when he left school on his fourteenth birthday in August.

Billy was in a dark angry mood after the new manager gave him his ultimation and when he went to school that day he was so disruptive that the student teacher banished him to stand outside the classroom for the time that remained before the lunch break.

Bagwash Billy seethed with red anger and decided to wag school and go home before the lunch bell rang but when he glanced down the stairwell to ensure the coast was clear he saw a chance to strike back at the world. A small blonde girl from his class had been delegated the job of stair monitor. She was a kid from the buildings and she stood alone and unprotected on the first floor landing armed with just a pencil and a monitor's notebook.

Billy made scary noises when he jumped the flight of stairs but when he loomed over his prey there was no fear in the huge blue eyes that calmly stared up at him.

'Walk down the rest of the stairs Billy or I'll write your name in the monitor book.'

The angel-faced twit had dared to challenge him. She needed to be taught respect. Billy pushed her back hard against the wall. He snatched her pencil away and snapped it in half.

Mick Doherty could have warned Billy that the angel-faced twit was fast, fearless and had a devastating kick but Mick Doherty was in class waiting for the clang of the lunch-time bell.

Big Bad Bagwash Billy had never been so swiftly disabled before. His scream of agony brought the headmaster running from his office. The headmaster sent for the science teacher to help him to carry Billy to the first-aid room where the school-nurse, who was more used to treating and consoling Bagwash Billy's victims, gave Billy no sympathy at all. The school nurse told the headmaster that as Billy's large head was undamaged that he should go home as soon as he was able to walk properly again and apply a cold compress to his damaged part.

The school nurse gave Kathy Henson two boiled sweets from her good child jar.

The headmaster took no further action after Billy insisted that he had fallen down the stairs in a complicated accident and to Mick's jealous annoyance and to my unease, Billy Bagwash worshipped Kathy from that day forward. No one had ever shown Billy the gentle care and quiet concern that the girl with the big blue eyes had shown him as he writhed in agony at the foot of the stairs.

When Kathy learned of Billy's inability to deal with simple invoices and receipt books and that he had until August to learn simple basic book-keeping skills to keep his delivery run she offered to tutor him on the proviso that he did not wag school on any of the remaining days that he had left as a student at the Sumner Road School.

Billy Bagwash accepted Kathy's offer and teachers were amazed and a touch nervous when he not only appeared on time at morning assembly every day but he was quieter and almost well behaved in the classrooms. Kathy used the lunch break and time after school to teach Billy basic reading and writing and simple bookkeeping.

Kathy was a good teacher and before the end of July Billy could copy and print a name on an invoice slip and he could proudly sign his own name legibly for the first time in his life.

That Bagwash Billy's mother was an alcoholic who paid a tiny rent to sleep with her two children in the basement of a small terraced house in Cator Street was common knowledge at the school but nobody knew the details of Billy's home life until he asked Kathy if she would tutor him in his basement home on days when he had to baby sit his sister and Kathy agreed.

I saw Bagwash Billy in a different light when Kathy described his homelife to me. The big basement in which he lived had only the basic utilities; a cold water tap over a double sink, two power-points and a gas-ring. Billy slept on a thin single mattress in one corner and his mother slept on a double mattress in another corner and Billy's baby sister slept in a big lidless suitcase beside Billy's mattress.

The family income came from Billy's laundry pick-up and delivery service supplemented by an occasional 'extra' from one of his mother's 'gentlemen friends'. His mother had no idea who had fathered either of her children and her fondness for gin meant that Billy was usually responsible for the feeding and care of his baby sister and until Kathy Henson kicked down the door to Billy's heart his baby sister had been the only living person to have known Billy's affection and Kathy was touched when Billy told her that his mother had granted his wish that his baby sister be named 'Kathy.'

Billy never once slacked off learning to read and write while Kathy was tutoring him and when he left school on his fourteenth birthday he could read the words on notice-boards and in newspapers. He also promised Kathy that he would join the public library and start reading books but Mick was not impressed. Mick was relieved when Bagwash Billy left school.

Billy had an appointment to with the new laundry manager on Sunday August 15th to learn if he had secured his delivery run and he was looking forward to showing the manager how far his reading and writing skills had progressed.

Billy promised Kathy that he would visit the school on Monday morning and tell her the outcome of the meeting and when he hadn't appeared by the mid-morning break Kathy was concerned. She was worried that something bad may have happened to Bagwash Billy during the night's heavy air-raid.

Mick had scowled and said, 'forget him Kathy, it's good riddance to the big bad rubbish.'

Kathy's fears were realised when Billy limped into the classroom as the lunch bell clanged. He was a terrible mess. Strips of adhesive tape held closed a ragged wound that ran down the right side of his face from the corner of his eye-brow to his jaw. He was barefoot, his clothes were plastered to his body by a sticky brown substance that exuded such a foul stench that it caused a fast exodus from the classroom until only the teacher, Kathy, Mick and I remained with Billy Bagwash.

Billy's mutilated face twisted into a parody of the rare smile that he only showed to Kathy, 'I'm sorry I'm late. I'm keeping my run...the new manager gave me lots of good ideas. I got some big plans...I might even be rich one day.'

Kathy ignored the nauseating filth on his clothes and took hold of his big hands. She went up on tip-toes and gently kissed the uninjured side of his face and said, 'I never believed that you would lose your run for one second Billy.' Then she looked down at his dirty bleeding feet, 'where are your boots?'

Billy frowned at his bloodied feet, 'I lost 'em. I can't find Mum either and a copper took baby Kathy away. Will you help me find my boots and my sister?'

The headmaster hurried into the class-room at that point. He was closely followed by two ambulance officers carrying a stretcher. One of the ambulance officers said in a loud genial voice, 'I didn't expect you to do a bolt to see your girl Bill. Climb aboard our chariot soldier and we'll get you washed up and into some clean clothes so that doctor can finish stitching up your face. Then I'll give you a free ride on the chariot to see your baby sister.'

Kathy gently steered Billy towards them, 'don't worry Billy – you go to the hospital with the ambulance men and I'll come and find you and little Kathy there.'

Looking dazed, Billy obediently nodded and he allowed the ambulance officers to help him lie down on the stretcher and he was carried out of the classroom. That was the last time that I saw Bagwash Billy.

The next day everybody was talking about the bravery of Bagwash Billy. A bomb had struck his house in the early hours of the morning and another had hit the roadway outside. Police and ARP wardens were unaware that anyone was in the basement and six hours passed before a passer-by in the street heard a baby's faint cries coming from under the debris of the house where it was believed that every occupant had died.

The second bomb that hit the roadway had breached the sewer main in the street and when the rubble was shifted so that the A.R.P wardens could enter the basement they saw Bagwash Billy standing neck-deep in filth holding a crying baby above his head to breathe the less than ten inches of stale air that remained between the rising sewage and the basement's low roof. He had stood for hours in total blackness holding his sister up to the diminishing air space.

Twenty years later I looked with misting eyes at the photograph of a celebrity wedding and I wished that somehow Kathy was aware of the miracle that she had helped to create on the other side of the world.

11

1943
separation

The heavy rain that began falling on London in late September continued without let-up until the end of October and cold rains of October were followed by cold fogs of November. Viruses had a field-day in chilly damp London and pneumonia developed in Kathy's weak lungs after a bout of influenza and Dr Cohen ordered strict bed-rest for Kathy until her high temperature subsided and no return to school until he gave his permission.

We had been transferred at the beginning of the year to Oliver Goldsmith School on the corner of Peckham High Street and Southampton Way and Mick and I missed Kathy's lively chatter on our longer walk to and from school. Daytime air-raids were not occurring as often as they did in the Blitz although enemy planes still came at night and disturbed our sleep with high explosive bombs and bundles of incendiaries.

We were twelve years old and aware that a rubble filled bomb-site or crater in a street of houses marked the place where people may have died; we had grown up and learned that we were not immortal. Every morning Mick and I walked to school along streets littered with shrapnel and debris from the previous night's air-raids. The interiors of bomb blasted houses were exposed as though giants had peeled back the walls to create dioramas of family life.

As soon as Kathy could leave her bed and cook her own meals Gloria Henson gave her flat-key to Maureen Doherty and ignoring Gran Doherty's pointed remarks Gloria returned to her club hostess work.

Kathy's father was overseas and at the first faint wails of a distant siren in the night Mick and Danny would grab the key to the Henson flat and race upstairs. If Gloria wasn't home, as was usually the case, the boys would over-ride Kathy's protests and forcibly escort her down to the shelter wrapped in a blanket. If she objected too strongly they would threaten to carry her. After weeks of this unsatisfactory routine Maureen decided to return to the Blitz sleeping arrangement we had in the Blitz and Kathy, Mick and I went back to reporting to Maureen at sunset every night and sleeping in the communal shelter.

The shelters for the Sumner Road Estate were partially buried in grassed areas behind the blocks of flats on Sumner Road and when grass grew over the shelters the long green mounds resembled ancient burial barrows – a disturbing image when a direct bomb hit on any one of the surrounding five-story blocks of flats would bring down an avalanche of bricks and bury hundreds of tenants sleeping in the communal shelter below.

Floors in the communal shelters were cement and furnishing was minimal: bench seats and tiered narrow wooden bunk beds with thin kapok mattresses. Cold-water taps over long stone troughs provided water for drinking and iron buckets in discreetly curtained alcoves took care of calls of Nature. Candles and paraffin-oil stoves were permitted although both paraffin-oil and candle wax became scarce and ran out as the war progressed.

Kathy slept in the bunk below mine and she found sleep impossible until Mick and I made up a wide bed on the floor with our bunk mattresses and Kathy slept cosily cuddled between us. Gran likened us to three puppies snuggled in a litter.

Kathy was a talented artist and during the weeks she was absent from school she occupied herself by creating Christmas gifts and cards and she designed a very special Christmas card for her marine commando father. First she sewed two squares of stiff lavender paper together with gold thread and glittering ice-crystals decorated the tiny green holly leaves on the card's scalloped edges. On the frontispiece a snowman stood in deep glistening snow in front of a dark green holly bush covered with bright red berries and a perky robin redbreast perched on the iced brim of the snowman's jaunty top hat. Heart shaped dabs of bright white snow on the leaves of the dark green holly bush spelled the message "Merry Xmas".

Kathy drew a pen and ink self-portrait inside the card that looked more like her than her school photo. The card was to go into a parcel for her father together with a scarf Kathy was knitting from recycled wool, paper-back books that her father liked to read and a packet of hard to get ready-rubbed tobacco that Gloria had bought from a black marketeer.

Christmas parcels for troops serving overseas had to be packed in special boxes and left at the local W.V.S. office before the first of December. At end of October Kathy had not quite finished knitting her Dad's scarf nor had she penned a message in his card when an official telegram from the War Office was delivered to the Henson flat bearing the shocking news that Kathy's adored hero father had been killed fighting in Italy.

Gloria Henson recovered quickly from the loss of her husband with the keen support of the manager of the club where she worked but Kathy was inconsolable and pneumonia returned to inflame her lungs. Kathy was critically ill when Dr Cohen tried to admit her to hospital but all the London hospitals were so over-crowded with war and civilian causalities that patients were being nursed in the corridors. Dr Cohen bullied Gloria Henson into staying home from the club to nurse Kathy in the shelter. Gloria did not make a very good nurse and Dr Cohen took Kathy off complete bed-rest when her temperature began to subside and Gloria Henson returned to her club work as soon as her daughter could prepare her own food.

Everyone was concerned by Kathy's low spirits although Gloria dismissed out of hand any suggestion that Kathy was deeply depressed.

During the day Kathy moped around her empty flat like a small frail lonely ghost and when we came home from school not even Mick's frenetic comic antics could coax her to smile and then Dr Cohen shocked all of us when he told Gloria Henson that he had arranged six weeks convalescence for Kathy at his widowed aunt's small farm in East Anglia.

Our trio had never been apart for longer than a few

days before and Mick and I loudly protested against sending Kathy away to live in a strange place with strangers.

'A holiday in the country with farm animals is just what Kathy needs to get well and be happy again,' Dr Cohen said when he tried hard to reassure me and Mick.

'bollocks! I'm going wiv 'er. Kathy will need me to protect her from the big farm animals like a mad bull.'

'Nonsense, every creature that moves on four legs or wears fur or feathers, loves Kathy. There isn't a carthorse in Peckham that doesn't greet her and expect a tidbit from her pocket when she passes on the street. She knows the name of every single horse in the local stables. Besides the most dangerous creature on Aunt Mabel's farm is a self-important gander with attitude called Himmler.'

Kathy was still lost in her black depression and showed no interest whatsoever in the plan to send her away and it was left to me and Mick to extract promises from both Doctor Cohen and Maureen that we would be re-united with Kathy for Christmas.

I gave Kathy a school exercise book and begged her to keep a daily journal while she was away because Mick and I wanted to know everything about the farm and the name of every person she met and every single thing that happened to her. Mick and I pasted a photo of the three of us on the front of the exercise book to constantly remind her of us.

Kathy didn't forget Mick and me. She filled the exercise book with her farm adventures and I have shared her exciting story here under the title…"Kathy's Story"

12

1943
Kathy's story

Kathy was still numb with grief when she arrived at the Cohen Farm and was met by the doctor's plump aunt. Kathy expected to hear the usual platitudes when she said, 'thank you for having me Mrs Cohen,' but Mabel Cohen quietly asked, 'who is Mrs Cohen? I am your Aunt Mabel.

Mabel Cohen had opened wide her large plump arms and cocooned the frail unhappy girl in a much needed long warm embrace that lasted until Kathy broke down in a torrent of healing tears and in between deep sobs and gulping breaths Kathy bared her grieving heart to Mabel Cohen and the dark shadows in which she had been lost for weeks dissolved away and she even showed Aunt Mabel the Christmas card that she had made for her father.

Kathy went to bed that night in a warm cosy attic that smelled faintly of ripening apples and for the first time in many weeks she slept deeply with her hand on her father's card that had been tucked underneath her pillow by kindly Aunt Mabel.

Mabel Cohen trusted the crisp clean air of East Anglia to heal Kathy's damaged lungs and the farm's wholesome food to nourish her frail body. To mend her young charge's depression she gave Kathy a lot of affection and kept the sorrowing girl fully occupied with light duties about the farm that gave Kathy little time to brood but more importantly made her feel useful and appreciated. On day two Mabel Cohen was thrilled when Kathy addressed her without hesitation as 'Aunt Mabel'.

Dr Cohen had made a correct prediction when he said that the farm animals would prove a never ending source delight for animal-lover Kathy. It was love at first sight between Kathy and the farm dog an aged English-sheepdog misnamed Biter and Kathy soon forged a good rapport with Elsa the temperamental nanny-goat and with Bob the pony who pulled the light trap that provided transport for Aunt Mabel without using the farm's precious stock of petrol. Bob learned very quickly to nuzzle Kathy's pockets for a tidbit of apple or carrot. The farm's free-ranging ducks came quaking when Kathy called them at feeding times.

Kathy's relationship was not so good with Himmler a big gander that strutted about the farm with his gaggle of geese but then Himmler had never met a human leg that he didn't want to attack.

Hard working Mabel Cohen reminded Kathy of a genteel Maureen Doherty. War caused a shortage of able bodied farm-workers and Mabel Cohen ran her small farm with the help of Joe, an experienced farmhand in his eighties who had volunteered to come out of retirement to work for the Cohen farm and Beth, an exuberant Land Army girl assigned to Mabel Cohen by the Government.

Kathy had instantly bonded with friendly boisterous Beth who rode a noisy two-stroke motor-cycle around the farm and spoke with a Scottish accent. Kathy enjoyed doing her light tasks about the peaceful farm and although she kept her father's Christmas card in her pocket during the daytime and under her pillow at night the sadness in her heart began to ease.

The countryside around the farm was marshy fenland and one could see for miles. In her free hours Kathy would sit on a low wall of weathered stones that surrounded the farmhouse and look across the hoar frosted fields that stretched to the North Sea on the eastern horizon. Far off to the west a river was a silver ribbon that meandered through the fens until it joined the North Sea. As Kathy's health inproved she began to miss Nell and Mick.

Mrs Cohen had confided the tragic reason for Kathy's sadness to Beth and the Land Army girl went out of her way to raise Kathy's spirits. On the fifth day of Kathy's stay at the farm Beth invited Kathy to ride on the motorbike with her when she went across the frosted fields to check the thickness of ice forming on the river. Beth had joked with her cheeky grin.'Of course the pony and trap are always available if you'd rather go on a wild shopping spree in the village shop with Mrs Cohen.'

'I've seen the village shop but I've never had a ride on a motorbike.'

'A motor-bike is the only way to travel. Climb aboard Princess and hang on.'

When Beth brought her bright-eyed and red-cheeked passenger back to the farm an hour later Kathy talked with animation about tall water reeds frozen stiff at the river's edge and strange birds with haunting cries but what gave Kathy the biggest thrill was Beth's offer to teach her to ice-skate if the pond close to the river froze solid. Beth had a local friend with children who would lend Kathy a small pair of boots with ice-skates attached.

Mabel Cohen telephoned her nephew in London that evening to tell him that his young patient had begun to heal in mind as well as body. Kathy still kept her father's Christmas card close and she continued to knit the long scarf until her wool ran out but she had put sorrow to one side and was smiling again.

Kathy's favourite chore at the farm was preparing the morning and afternoon teas. Gloria Henson's poor mothering had resulted in her daughter becoming a good cook and Kathy soon mastered the peat-fired range in the farmhouse kitchen. Her only regret was that ever-hungry Mick in tightly rationed London would never see the abundance of eggs, butter, cheese and preserves on the shelves of the farm's big walk-in pantry.

On her tenth morning at the farm Kathy placed a large platter of freshly baked scones on the long scrubbed kitchen table together with a dish of freshly churned butter, a jug of cream, a jar of homemade strawberry jam and a pot of honey from the farm's bee-hives. She baked extra scones that morning because Aunt Mabel had alerted her that as well as Beth and old Joe a casual farm-hand would join them for morning tea.

'That table looks absolutely scrumptious. I only hope my farm-workers don't expect home cooking as good as this for their morning and afternoon teas after you return to London. The young man that you marry will be a very lucky young fellow indeed.' Mabel Cohen had then opened wide the kitchen window and called to somebody chopping firewood outside, 'we are having have fresh baked scones with honey, strawberry jam and fresh cream for our morning tea, Bruno – will you join us?'

'Grazie – Senora,' and seconds later the back door opened and a short stocky man with thick black curling hair stood on the coir mat in the doorway stamping snow from his boots. His shirt and trousers were made from a coarse brown cloth and covered with large irregular brightly coloured patches. His dark brown eyes rested on Kathy and he smiled and spoke with foreign accent, 'good morning signorina, snow is falling thickly outside.'

'Kathy, this is Bruno Rossi. Bruno will be working on the farm until Christmas.'

Kathy backed slowly across the kitchen staring at the man in silent shocked disbelief and when she reached the open doorway that led to the inner wooden staircase she turned and ran stumbling up the narrow stairs to her attic bedroom.

Kathy curled into a foetal ball on the bed with her face to the wall. She had recognised the strange clothes worn by the dark-eyed man downstairs in the kitchen. Bruno was a prisoner of war on work leave – he was on of the enemy from Italy who had killed her Dad.

She smelled the sharp clean fragrance of lavender water and the deep feather mattress moved under the weight of Aunt Mabel's body.

'Sit up child and look at me. I want to talk to you about Bruno.'

Kathy tightly clutched her father's Christmas card and remained silent as she whirled lost in a vortex of emotion. She heard again her father's laughter when he swung her squealing high above his head and she brimmed with hatred for the enemy downstairs in the kitchen.

'Kathy, until you catch the train back to London on Christmas Eve I insist that you show Bruno Rossi the same respect that you show to me and everybody else on the Cohen farm.'

Kathy sat up and Mabel sighed when she saw the young girl's cold closed face.

'Listen to me, Kathy. He was a medical orderly in a field hospital in North Africa when he was captured. It was not Bruno's choice to be a soldie...Bruno hates war. Italy surrendered weeks ago but there is fierce fighting between German and Allied soldiers in the part of Italy where Bruno's family live and he has had no news of his family for months.'

Kathy wasn't listening. In two weeks time she would be on a steam train speeding away from her enemy. She answered in a quiet voice, 'I'll be polite to him for your sade Aunt Mabel but I won't say his wop name – I'll call him Enemy.'

Mrs Cohen looked into Kathy's defiant blue eyes and knew the grief stricken girl would give no further concession.

Kathy avoided Bruno Rossi for two days by going outside whenever he came inside but Aunt Mabel insisted on Kathy remaining inside when the snow heavy clouds hung low over the snow covered fields and the air outside the warm farmhouse became freezing and just breathing was almost too painful for Kathy's weak lungs.

Open fires in the bedrooms were not lighted until nightfall to conserve the farm's meagre ration of coal and coke and after finishing her chores Kathy sat in the kitchen in front of the warm range and continued knitting the scarf she had intended for her father. She had reached the end of her wool supply but Aunt Mabel had searched out old knitted jumpers for Kathy to unpick into balls of coloured wool and knit into the scarf.

A spell of freezing cold weather is a good time on a farm to catch up with indoor work and Bruno Rossi, a carpenter in civilian life, was building wall shelves in the farmhouse kitchen. Kathy concentrated on her knitting and ignored the enemy working at the far end of the big kitchen but Bruno Rossi stole occasional troubled glances at the impassive golden haired girl knitting in front of the warm kitchen-range.

On the second day of the big freeze Kathy knitted as industriously as ever beside the warm kitchen range and as usual ignored her enemy. She had begun to knit a ball of bright red wool into the ever lengthening scarf when she felt a tug on the knitting needles. She looked down on the balls of wool by her feet and cried out with delight. Entangled in the ball of red wool was a small grey kitten. The baby cat mewed plaintively up at her and Kathy knelt on the floor and disentangled the kitten from the ball of wool. 'Where did this cat come from?'

The Enemy was humming to himself and was so engrossed in his work that he didn't hear her so Kathy spoke louder, 'did you see where this cat came from?'

Bruno glanced up at the kitchen door, he shrugged and went back to sanding a shelf.

Kathy scowled and raised her voice even louder, 'Hey! Enemy – are you bleeding deaf?'

Bruno Rossi looked a polite inquiry in her direction, 'do you speak Signorina Kathy?'

'Yeah – I asked if you knew that there's a strange cat in here.'

'Mamma Mia!' and before she could protest or retreat Bruno Rossi had swiftly crossed the room and knelt in front of her. Kathy shrank back; it was the closest that she had been to him.

'The bad boy escaped from my toolbox!' His dark brown eyes pleaded, 'we beg for your mercy Signorina Kathy. He is a stray baby with no mama and he would die out in the snow but it is forbidden to keep pets in the camp. If the guards see him they will shoot him.'

'Don't talk daft – he's too little to shoot.'

Kathy remembered Miss Tibbles and her voice became less belligerent, 'cats ain't allowed in the buildings where I live. What's his name then?'

'Aah his name. His name is another problem for me. I know many fine Italian names but somehow they do not seem right for him.'

'I should think not!' Kathy bristled. 'He's a British cat.' She looked closely at the kitten purring in her hands and a small velvet paw softly batted her cheek.

The Enemy sounded pensive, 'I could of course simply call him Gatto – that means…'

'I know what that means; that's a wop name for a tom-cat – a rotten name. If he was mine I'd call him Monty after General Montgomery. Monty is the bravest and the best general in the war in North Africa.' Big blue eyes fiercely challenged deep brown eyes.

Bruno pursed his lips and considered Kathy's suggestion for a full minute before nodding his approval, 'Si, Monty is a fine name and General Montgomery is a brave and honourable soldier. The problem is solved. The little cat is named Monty. '

Kathy held the purring kitten against her cheek and whispered, 'did you hear what Enemy just said? He has named you after Monty.'

'Signorina Kathy, I'm fear to ask but do you think

that you could care for Monty until you return to London? I need just a few days to find him a kind home in the village.'

Kathy tried to feel outrage that the Enemy had dared to ask for her help but the soft grey paw lightly batted her cheek again. 'Well…maybe I will. But only if Aunt Mabel likes cats in her house and she gives us her okay.'

'Then we go this very instant to ask the good Senora Cohen for her okay.'

Mabel Cohen raised her eyebrows when Bruno and Kathy approached her with hostilities apparently suspended as they seriously discussed what appeared to be a mutual problem with a fluffy grey kitten nestled in Kathy's thin arms.

Mabel instantly recognised the kitten as being one of the litter recently born to the village baker's pedigreed Siamese and as she listened to Bruno and Kathy's combined pleas for her to give the kitten temporary sanctuary at the farm Mabel wondered how much of his labour Bruno Rossi had bartered for the expensive pretty feline.

Kathy begged, 'Please say Monty can stay at the farm for a while Aunt Mabel. He won't be any trouble. I promise that I'll care for him until Christmas Eve when I go home. He is so beautiful, I'm sure that Enemy will find him a good home in the village by then.'

'Bruno, why did you name the kitten Monty?' Mabel Cohen asked.

'It was Kathy who suggested the name of the brave General Montgomery.'

'Of course it was Kathy's idea.' Mabel Cohen smiled and gave Bruno a surreptitious wink when she took the kitten out of Kathy's hands. 'Monty seems to be in excellent shape, Puddy the farm's cat died of old age in the summer so if you are both agreeable Monty can take the late Puddy's place as Cohen farm's official mouser.'

Kathy was overjoyed.

Mabel Cohen soon realised the Italian's ploy to use the kitten to thaw the ice in Kathy's heart had been a brilliant strategy. The kitten became a bridge between Kathy and her Enemy. She listened to Bruno's stories about his family and his family's small house in a village of painted stone houses that sprawled on the gentle slopes of a sun-washed hill in southern Italy. Bruno showed her a photo of his wife Maria holding their baby Anna and with their twin sons Antonio and Alphonse standing beside her and they were all smiling at the camera.

Within a day or two Kathy was giggling at funny anecdotes Bruno told about Mimi, the Rossi family's wayward nanny-goat although she never shared any details of her personal life and Aunt Mabel failed to persuade Kathy to use Bruno's proper name. He remained 'Enemy' for stubborn Kathy and she didn't tell Aunt Mabel or anyone else at the farm that prayers for the safety of Maria Rossi and her children had crept into her nightly prayers.

Caring for the kitten made time fly and Kathy woke early one cold morning surprised by the realisation that the next day was Christmas Eve. Kathy had wanted to go home so much that she was surprised that the thought of leaving Aunt Mabel, Beth and old Joe made her sad and saying goodbye to Biter and Monty was going to be especially difficult.

When Kathy went down stairs she found herself alone in the farmhouse. A note from Aunt Mabel was on the kitchen table asking her to make her own breakfast. Aunt Mabel had been called out early to help a neighbour in trouble and she had taken Beth with her.

Kathy ate breakfast and poured milk into Monty's dish before she put on her warmest coat and gloves to go outside and ask old Joe if he knew anything about the emergency that had called Aunt Mabel and Beth out into the cold so early in the morning. She found Joe mucking out the pony's stable and he told her that there had been a bad accident on the neighbouring farm and Mrs Cohen and Beth were using the pony and trap to take the injured farm worker to hospital in the nearby town. Mrs Cohen had left a message for Kathy that she and Beth would return home in time for morning tea.

When Kathy returned to the kitchen she noticed the milk in Monty's dish was untouched. She went outside again and whistled for Biter. The old dog had formed an unlikely alliance with Monty and had shown no objection to being tagged everywhere he went by the tiny newcomer. When Biter didn't respond to her whistles and shouts Kathy assumed that he and Monty were cosily snuggled together in a sheltered nook protected from the east wind.

Kathy sat on the low stone wall by the front gate from where she could keep watch on the road for the pony and trap. She stared across the flat expanse of whitened fields to the silver river and wondered if the small pond was frozen solid enough for ice skating. She wanted to take an ice skating story home to Nell and Mick tomorrow. She was sure that they missed her as much as she missed them. The three of them had never been apart for this length of time before. Kathy reached into her coat pocket and took out her father's card. The weeks at the farm had blunted the sharp sorrow of her father's death to a bearable ache and she could now look at the snowman on the front of the card without tears.

Kathy returned the Christmas card to her pocket and resumed watching for the pony and trap's appearance on the distant road that would be her cue to put the kettle on. She could see a lone cyclist on the road from the village and she wondered if the cyclist was Enemy on his way to work at the farm.

A dog had been barking near the river for some time, that the barking dog might be Biter had struck Kathy as a fanciful idea but some fanciful ideas do turn out to be true and when the distant barks changed to mournful howls she climbed on to the top of the wall and looked toward the river. The dog was out of her sight but if the animal now howling a lament was Biter then Monty could be in danger because wherever Biter went Monty followed and the kitten would surely die in the icy wind knifing across the frosty fields from the North Sea.

Once doubt had taken hold of Kathy she didn't hesitate; she jumped off the wall and plodded through the deep snow towards the river and the howling dog.

She could only move as fast as the deep snow and her heavy winter clothing would permit.The canine howls grew louder the closer Kathy came to the river and sharp pains stabbed her chest as her weak lungs strained to breathe the refrigerated air.

When Kathy finally reached the river she saw Biter standing hock-deep in icy slush in a clump of stiff frozen reeds at the water's edge. As soon as the old sheep-dog became aware of her presence his mournful howls changed to relieved whimpers.

Kathy dropped to her knees in the ice slush and hugged the wet bedraggled dog. 'Good boy. Where's your chum? Where's Monty?'

Biter turned his shaggy head and looked toward the river. Kathy cried out in horrified alarm when she saw the tiny ball of sodden grey fur on a small square of floating ice that had broken away from the wide apron of ice attached to the riverbank.

Monty miaowed when he saw Kathy. The fast river current was jostling loose pieces of ice together and threatening the kitten's precarious hold on the slippery piece of ice.

Kathy tried to coax Monty on to the apron of ice that still clung to the river bank and when his forepaws dipped into the icy river water he scrambled to the back of his tiny ice-raft with piteous mews of fear.

Kathy tried talking sternly to the terrified kitten, 'Monty get off that silly little bit of ice at once and come to me.'

Monty miaowed even louder when his square of loose ice began bumping against the shelf of ice frozen to the river bank and Kathy forced herself to remain calm. She cautiously tested the ice shelf protruding from the bank and discovered that it supported her light weight. She gingerly crawled across the ice-shelf until she was close enough to grab hold of Monty who monitored her approach with frightened eyes but as Kathy reached out to grasp him the shelf of ice cracked at the edge of the bank and tilted beneath her. Kathy screamed as she plunged into the cold river. A powerful current swept her underneath the neighbouring ice shelf.

It was her terror that woke Kathy from a drowning nightmare in a blue shadowed ice cave beneath solid ice and she woke to a reality that she was safe and warm in her soft bed in the farm's attic bedroom. A small peat fire burned in the open grate and warm and dry Monty loudly purred on her pillow.

Kathy was confused. Monty had been in icy peril floating on the frigid river but his soft grey coat was fluffy dry, 'I had a really bad dream that you were boating on a raft of ice and I was...' her mind was clearing and Kathy knew the freezing river water and being trapped in a blue cavern underneath the river ice were not nightmares, they were real as were the strong hands that lifted her out of the river and Biter washing her cold face with his slobbery warm tongue had been real as she lay on snow wrapped in a warm coat that smelt of garlic and tobacco. She remembered Biter's whimpers and a voice muttering strange words in what sounded like desperate prayers before fading away as she fell into silent blackness.

Monty wormed his way under the bed-covers to share her warmth and Kathy dragged the kitten out from where he was trying to snuggle under her legs. 'Come out of there, you silly little sod – I hope you've thanked Biter…'

Kathy started at Biter's short bark, normally barred from the upstairs rooms the old dog was stretched out on the hand-made rag-rug beside her bed and Kathy leaned down to rub his head and was surprised to hear Aunt Mabel's voice.

'How do you feel Kathy? I do believe that you have slept for over six hours.'

Mabel Cohen sat in a rocker-chair on the other side of the bed knitting a ball of pale blue wool into Kathy's really long multi-coloured scarf.

'I'm so sorry Aunt Mabel.' Kathy's blue eyes were brilliant with unshed tears, 'honest I am. I had no right to get into a pickle and worry you. I was scared that Monty would drown.'

'Don't fret dear. Bruno told us what happened at the river. We all think that you were a very brave girl to try to save Monty – foolish perhaps – but still very brave.'

Mabel Cohen looked critically at her knitting, 'This scarf will take the record for being the longest scarf in the British Isles but I couldn't sit here with idle hands for six hours.'

Kathy sank back into feather filled pillows and Monty purred hoarsely as he stalked across the low hill of her stomach. Kathy gently rubbed his ears, 'I thought I saw the Enemy riding his bike along the road coming from the village.'

'That's right, you did see Bruno and if you had looked back when you reached the river you would have seen him cycling across the field on his way to help you.'

'He pulled me out of the river…didn't he?'

'Bruno had to swim under the ice twice before he found you and when he brought you up on to the bank you had stopped breathing. Luckily for you Bruno had been a medical orderly during the war and knew how to perform artificial respiration and make you breathe again. Bruno's bicycle doesn't have a cross-bar and you were unconscious so he wrapped you in his overcoat and ran all the way to the farmhouse holding you in his arms.'

Kathy's blue eyes were pensive, 'did Monty get off the floating ice by himself?'

'Bruno returned to the river and went back into the icy water again and rescued Monty. I had already sent Beth in the trap to bring Dr Haynes. I tried to persuade

Bruno to wait for Beth to return with the trap or at least change out of his wet clothes before he went out into the cold again but he didn't want you to suffer the loss of another loved one – even if the loved one was only a naughty little kitten.'

Kathy remained silent for several minutes and then she said in a matter of fact voice, 'he was wounded in North Africa and only one of his lungs works; he was bleeding barmy to jump back into that freezing river. What happened to Enemy after he saved Monty?'

'Beth took Bruno back to camp in the pony and trap and the camp doctor admitted him to the camp hospital on bed-rest.'

'Is Enemy okay now?'

'I telephoned the camp doctor and was told that Bruno should be fine after a few days bed rest. Don't you think now that you could call Bruno by his proper name?'

Kathy stayed silent. Her vivid blue eyes were on the small ball of grey fur purring beneath her caressing hand. Mabel Cohen sighed and she gave up trying to thaw Kathy's frosty heart. 'Dr Haynes ordered that you stay in bed for the rest of today – you'll have a tiring train trip back to London tomorrow. I've left you a hand-bell that you can ring if you need anything. Beth will come up in an hour or so and keep you company. She's going to bring you her sketching pad and charcoals. Is there anything that I can get for you right now?'

'Do you know where my coat is? I had something important in the zipped pocket.'

Mabel Cohen nodded, 'your coat is drying in front of the range in the kitchen so that you can wear it on the train tomorrow. The Christmas card in the coat pocket survived a dunking in the river although it is stained and damp, I've put it on the bedside table beside you.'

'Ta ever so much, Aunt Mabel,' Kathy said in a small quiet voice.

Christmas Day dawned snowy and cold. Corporal Bruno Rossi was confined to a bed in the prison camp hospital but he was at peace. The pains in his chest had subsided and the most effective medicine of all for Bruno Rossi was the news that the International Red Cross had located his family safe and well in Italy and Christmas greetings had been exchanged each way and if recent news bulletins were not just Allied propaganda there was renewed optimism among the Italian prisoners at the camp that the end of the war was near.

Bruno smiled when his eyes rested on a large cane laundry hamper on the floor at the foot of his bed. Old Joe had delivered the hamper yesterday.The hard-working Italians at the camp had made many friends locally. The hamper had been packed with knitted mittens, scarves and socks, a second-hand serviceable wind-up phonograph record player with records. There were books, packs of playing cards and farm food – fresh eggs, butter, cheese and herbs were welcomed by the camp's Italian cooks.

Draped across Bruno's broad shoulders was a long multi-coloured scarf that would have given the biblical Joseph's coat a run for having the most colours. Bruno felt that he had found hidden treasure when he found the incredibly long woollen scarf gift wrapped at the bottom of the hamper with his name boldly printed on recycled Christmas wrapping paper but the real hidden treasure for Bruno was the water stained hand-painted Christmas card that he found tucked into the innermost fold of the colourful scarf. A snow scene complete with a snowman and a holly bush decorated the front of the card and pasted on the inside pages was a lifelike pen and ink sketch of a smiling Kathy and a charcoal image of a blue-eyed Siamese kitten that closely resembled Monty. Bruno knew the tragic history of the crumpled but still beautiful Christmas card. His brown eyes misted every time he read the card's neatly printed message: Dear Enemy, we wish you a Happy Christmas, we love you…Kathy and Monty xx

13

three fond memories

Six years of war in childhood gifted me with many memories of unforgettable people and incidents, far too many for this short childhood memoir. I have selected three true memories from the area in South East London where Kathy, Mick and I lived during the war years.

Memory one...a butterfly vs a traitor

i9The exotic butterfly in this true memory has large dark reddish-brown wings edged with bright sapphire-blue spots and a ruffled creamy-white fringe reminiscent of a lady's lacy petticoat. The beautiful butterfly is not native to Britain but it is a strong flyer and in the 1700s one was found in an alley in Camberwell and British entomologists of the day named the rare visitor the Camberwell Beauty. The lovely insect is known by other names overseas

In 1912 the paper manufacturing company Samuel Jones & Co. built a large five storied factory and paper mill in Southampton Way on the border of Peckham and Camberwell and adopted the Camberwell Beauty for the company logo. A giant glittering mosaic mural of the beautiful butterfly was erected on top of the façade of the new paper-mill. The shining mosaic butterfly could be seen for miles and brought a touch of much needed colour to the drab back streets of Camberwell and neighbouring Peckham.

The traitor in this memory is British born William Joyce, a Nazi sympathiser in World War Two who was given the nickname Lord Haw-Haw because of the phoney upper-class British accent he adopted to broadcast propaganda on his English speaking program on the wireless *This is Germany Calling.*

The audacious claims made by Lord Haw-Haw about the progress of the war and that Herr Adolf Hitler was a great man of peace and vision and that the British should put down their guns and embrace the world plans of the great Fuehrer amused listeners in Britain but he also had the power to unsettle some Britons with his intimate knowledge and up to date news of their neighbourhoods.

My father believed that any lie sounded true if said loudly and repeated often enough and he never allowed our wireless to be tuned to the European wavelength unless he was present. If I wanted to laugh at Lord Haw-Haw then I had to listen to him on the Doherty's wireless.

Gran Doherty always listened to Lord Haw-Haw and she would shout insults at the wireless and call him a liar. Gran shouted insults especially loudly the night Lord Haw-Haw boasted that Luftwaffe bomber pilots were the best in the world and that night they would prove their superior flying skills by destroying the giant sign of a butterfly on a factory roof in south-east London.

Early the next morning when Kathy, Mick and I woke up in the shelter we saw Gran was crying as she listened to a B.B.C. news bulletin on the wireless. She told us that the Samuel Jones factory in Southampton Way had been fire-bombed with incendiaries and destroyed during the night...on this occasion Lord Haw-Haw seemed to have told the truth.

Maureen was so moved by our unhappy faces that when the All Clear sirens sounded she gave us permission to ride our bicycles to the remains of the factory in Southampton Way. We all wanted to pick up a piece of the glittering mosaic sign as a memento of the beautiful butterfly.

We cycled down Southampton Way in company with dozens of solemn men, women and children on bicycles, roller-skates or on foot. Everybody was hurrying to the paper factory to look at the terrible sight of their beautiful butterfly utterly destroyed.

Tons of incendiaries had rained down on the big Samuel Jones factory during the night and the five story building was gutted. Here and there smoky spot fires still burned and the charred paper ash was still drifting down like black snow. The burnt paper ash had combined with water from the firefighter's hoses to create a black river of pulped paper on the stretch of roadway in front of the burnt out factory. The people in the crowd were staring at a desolate scene that should have brought tears to many but there was no sadness in anyone's face.

The eyes of the exhausted fire-fighters and the eyes of the smiling onlookers constantly gazed up through thick choking smoke to a giant mosaic butterfly still proudly upright on the charred roof-beams of the fire gutted factory. The golden rays of the rising sun accentuated the glowing colours on the Camberwell Beauty's defiantly outstretched wings.

The glittering mosaic of the Camberwell Beauty remained upright on the top of the fire gutted factory facade defying the enemy and lifting local spirits until the end of the war.

The mosaic of the beautiful butterfly that once graced the façade of Samuel Jones paper factory has been preserved in a public venue in Camberwell and is a treasured part of local war history shared by the residents of Camberwell and Peckham. A traitor lost his credibility the day he lost a propaganda fight with a beautiful butterfly.

Memory two...the naked canary

The winter of 1940/41 was miserably cold and when windy March roared in with promises of warm weather following I was imbued with thoughts of sunshine on spring-flowers and I decided to brighten the flat with a special indoor-garden. I began searching for garden-pots to fill with tulips and daffodils. I believed that I had found the centrepiece of my indoor-garden when I spotted a large battered bird-cage in the debris on a bomb-site.

The wire sides of the big cage were twisted out of shape and the door was missing but the roomy cage was exactly what I needed. I filled the deep tray at the bottom with several inches of a quality potting-mix and I sprinkled an entire packet of mixed spring flower seeds over the dampened soil.

Dad hung the bird-cage on a strong hook screwed into the frame of the window in the front room and I felt confident that once the flower seeds began to sprout I would own my own Hanging Indoor Garden...how wrong I was.

The next morning I walked into the front room

and was greeted with a musical barrage of melodious whistling. A naked squatter had flown in during the night and taken possession of what was to have been the centrepiece of my Hanging Indoor Garden.

The intruder was a small cock-canary sitting in the middle of the big birdcage and apart from a few wisps on his wings he was sans feathers. I knew the naked interloper was a canary because a scorched feather on a drooping wing was a dirty yellow and he was a cock-canary because hen-canaries do not sing.

It was easy to see how the scrawny bird had got inside the flat, Dad insisted on at least one window left open a few inches at the top even on the coldest day in winter.

The invader had eaten most of the seed that I had spread so thickly on the loam and when I put my hand inside the cage to try to save what little seed remained the thief stabbed my hand with his small sharp beak and I decided to wait for my father to arrive home from work and pass eviction of the small greedy vulture over to him.

Dad came home exhausted after a busy night shift. He put his hand into the cage and the bird perched on his finger and softly cheeped. I didn't want Dad to bond with the invader while I was at school so I offered to take the naked bird down to the old lady who lived on the ground floor and kept a budgerigar a lonely prisoner in a tiny cage and Dad asked me what I would do with the featherless refugee if the old lady refused to give him asylum. Dad offered two choices...wring the bird's neck and flush his tiny body down the toilet or wring the bird's neck and drop his tiny body down the rubbish chute? I told him I would leave that decision to him. I didn't believe for one second that my kindly father had any intention of applying either solution to the avian pest but I was surprised when I came home from school that afternoon to find earth in the tray at the bottom of the cage had been replaced with clean newspaper. A saucer filled with bird-seed was beside a saucer of clean water in the cage and bird swing and two roosting perches had been improvised from wooden meat-skewers.

The featherless bird was not in his five-star hotel. I peeped into Dad's bedroom and saw the bald refugee dozing on the picture rail above my sleeping father's head. By the weekend the naked canary with attitude answered to the name "Joe" and became a member of my family and I never did get an Indoor Hanging Garden.

The missing door on the battered cage was never replaced and Joe was free to fly away at any time but the little vulture knew when he was well off and he chose to stay. Within a few short months soft daffodil-yellow feathers began to regrow over his naked body and although his right wing always drooped Joe could fly properly as well as sing like an angel.

I believe Joe was able to tell time too because he knew to the minute when Dad was due to finish his night shift. Joe would sit in the window opening and wait for Dad to cycle down Sumner Road and ring his bicycle bell. The bell was the signal for Joe to swoop down on Dad like a hunting falcon and hitch a ride home singing his heart out perched on Dad's cap.

My father made a clear distinction between ordinary German people who he had always liked and Adolf Hitler's gang of Nazi thugs and Dad had been pleased when the vet informed him that Joe was a German 'roller' canary. The 'roller' canaries are prized for their ability to sing softly and sweetly but Joe could whistle and sing piercingly loud too.

Joe was so smart he could differentiate between the undulating wailing of the Alert siren and the steady note of the All-Clear siren. The lid of the coal-box outside the front-room was always kept open just for Joe.

At the first faint sound of a distant Alert siren Joe became a yellow flash through the flat before he dived into the dark coal-box. The sound of a distant All-Clear siren was the signal for Joe to emerge and take up his favourite station on the open top of the front-room window where he would perform a thrilling duet with the local sirens.

Only after every siren wailed into silence would Joe stop singing and fastidiously preen his feathers to remove any coal-dust.

Joe became well-known in Sumner Road. The Alliance patrons were his biggest fans and drinkers would come out of the pub and stand on the footpath to listen to Joe's unique duet with the All-Clear sirens.

The special bond that Joe forged with my father lasted until Death gently claimed the feisty small bird in peaceful old-age long after the war had ended.

Despite his invasion and occupation of my hanging-garden Roller Joe has remained one of my fondest memories of Peckham.

Memory three...the local family pub

A stroll down Sumner Road from Peckham High Street to Trafalgar Avenue during the Second World War would take the stroller past a public house on nearly every street corner. The favourite watering-hole for the tenants on the Sumner Road Estate was the small family pub on the corner of Lisford Street and Sumner Road called the *Alliance.*

The *Alliance* was the epitome of the 'family pub' of

those times with gleaming brasses, bar counters of polished oak and well-padded bench seats set against the walls. The ladies usually favoured the small carpeted private-bar they sometimes call the snug where they sat and chatted with their friends at small tables. The men preferred the saloon-bar with linoleum underfoot, an upright piano and a well-used dart-board fixed to the wall.

During World War Two the *Alliance* was the venue for many bon-voyage parties for the young local warriors about to go into battle – too many of whom never came home again. In 1941 an embarkation party was held in the *Alliance* for two friends, a sailor and a soldier who had been at school together. Drunkenness was frowned upon in family pubs but at closing time a silly alcohol fuelled disagreement flared between the two friends over the ownership of a ten shilling note that had been left in change on the saloon-bar counter.

The *Alliance* publican had intervened and cut the disputed note in half. The homespun Solomon gave one half of the ten shilling note to the sailor and the other half to the soldier and he told each young man to keep his half safe until the war was ended and when they returned home they could have a drink together in the *Alliance* with the repaired ten bob note.

The two friends did come home safely from war and they celebrated their safe return in the *Alliance* with the licensee who matched the repaired bank-note with a note from the till.

The *Alliance* escaped serious bomb damage during the war years but was damaged by friendly fire some years after the war ended when an anti-aircraft shell that had been rendered 'safe and inactive' and was being used as a talking-point door-stop, predictably exploded.

14

1944
our spooky adventure

Despte a lurid imagination I was a pragmatic child and logic sat securely on my young shoulders. No monsters lurked in a dark alley to accost me and the ghost haunted house was a joke to play on gullible friends like Mick whose belief in the supernatural often exasperated me. I recall a memorable occasion when Mick was sure that a murderous Egyptian mummy was stalking him.

Mick's unshakeable belief in the occult was understandable when so many of his relatives believed in the existence of a supernatural being of one sort or another. Gran Doherty used to chill our blood with tales of a banshee that had followed the Doherty family to London when they moved from Dublin decades ago and when London County Council evicted the Doherty family from Lambeth and rehoused them in a flat on the Sumner Road Housing Estate in Peckham their banshee tagged along and made a home for itself on the roof of their block of flats on Sumner Road.

Gran was not amused when my curious logic

prompted me to ask what was keeping a ghastly eye on the Doherty clan still residing in Dublin while the family spook was haunting a roof top in Peckham. For the enlightenment of the reader who is not aware of Celtic occult beliefs, a banshee is a family's private haunt that shrieks and wails a warning of approaching death when the demise of a family member is imminent.

Kathy Henson straddled the fence between superstition and common sense. Kathy claimed disbelief in the supernatural but she never broke a superstition taboo and she also gave creepy places and creepy people a wide berth. I understood Kathy's sensible stance; it was Mick's unshakeable belief in 'things that go bump in the night' that irritated me so much I offered to give him my pocket compass which I greatly valued and he coveted if he and I ever saw a ghost together.

Mick Doherty claimed that compass in 1944 at the end of the week Kathy, Mick and I spent at a W.V.S. holiday camp in the lovely Chiltern Hills.

The tireless angels of the Women's Voluntary Service organised many inexpensive safe holidays for older children who lived in the heavily bombed cities and after stern warnings from my Dad and Maureen that we were not to repeat our evacuation misbehaviour Kathy, Mick and I were allowed to attend a week-long W.V.S. camping holiday in the Chiltern Hills.

Dad and Maureen had no cause for concern; we were no longer the ten year old kids that we had been in Lesser Dymwich. We would be teenagers in September – we were grown ups.

There were thirty or so children from London schools in our camping group and everyone was looking forward to a fun filled week with fresh air, singing around a camp fire and sleep all night undisturbed by an air-raid. Our group of young campers were chaperoned by three W.V.S ladies, who managed to be fun as well as strict. The ladies were aided by somebody's grumpy grandfather who volunteered to join the holiday to keep an eye on the boys.

Our boisterous group of twelve and thirteen year-old children was housed in three long Nissen huts sited in a field outside a small town in the Chiltern Hills. The grumpy grandfather and the boys slept in one hut, the girls and the three W.V.S ladies slept in another and the third hut was used as a communal meeting place for recreation and every other activity.

Directly opposite our campsite on the other side of a narrow dirt road was a small ancient church named St Jude. A red-brick vicarage was next door to the church and the vicarage's kitchen garden shared a low wall with the church graveyard. The vicar of St Jude and his family were unfailingly tolerant of the noisy campers from London on the other side of their quiet road and townspeople in the nearby town went out of their way to welcome us.

The only signs we saw of the war were fighter planes passing overhead that were based at a nearby air-field. Two days after our arrival boys from a local school challenged the London boys to a football match and planes returning to the nearby air-base during the robust game flew so low over the playing field that we identified the colourful 303 insignia of the greatly admired Free Polish Spitfire squadron painted on the bullet scarred fuselages.

The referee joined in our wild waving and cheering when one of the Spitfires returned and did two slow victory rolls low over our heads. The Spitfire buzzed us again and flew around the playing field at tree-top level. The Polish pilot didn't need to speak English to tell us that he had downed two enemy planes.

The group had such a great holiday that everybody felt a little sad when our week drew to a close. For the last day of the holiday the three W.V.S. ladies and the grumpy grandpa had planned a long hike in the local hills that finished with a picnic. All the adults were needed to supervise the large group of young hikers and this created a problem for Kathy, Mick and me. Although six months had passed since Kathy almost drowned under river ice in East Anglia she was still convalescent and strictly forbidden to undertake any activity that involved her in physical exertion and Mick and I flatly refused to be parted from Kathy for a whole day.

The problem was solved when the vicar and his wife offered to take Kathy, Mick and me under their wing for the day so that the W.V.S. ladies and grumpy grandpa would be free to escort the rest of the campers on the planned long hike in the hills.

Kathy, Mick and I had such a happy day at the vicarage that Kathy soon lost any guilt she felt over me and Mick missing out on a long hike through the hills and lunch was especially yummy with a strawberry jam tart for dessert baked especially for us by the vicar's wife. We also ate sweet gooseberries from a bush in the vicarage garden. The vicar's teenaged son, a likeable likely lad named Martin, topped off our day by taking us on a guided tour of ancient St Jude's church and its small graveyard. The historic church was interesting but we were enthralled by the graveyard. The graves were overgrown by grasses and trailing vines and the mossy headstones leaned at odd angles. The graves were so old that even Mick showed no signs of unease at being surrounded by dead people. The most recent date that he deciphered on a lichen coated headstone was 1836. The weather-stained stone and marble sculptures that seemed to adorn every grave were mostly chipped and broken.

The small cemetery reminded us of a neglected garden, the wildflowers of mid-summer had loaned the old burial ground an unkempt beauty but it was easy to imagine how starkly lonely it would look in leafless winter.

I remember the exact moment when my sneaky logic whispered in my ear that the old cemetery might offer me a chance to refute Mick's illogical beliefs. Mick and Kathy were kneeling on the grass with their backs to me as they deciphered the weather-worn words on a marble tablet held in the chipped fingers of a stone angel sitting with folded wings beside a double grave in the centre of the cemetery. I even remember thinking that I would clip the wings of the banshee some other time.

I winked at Martin and I could not have sounded more casual when I said, 'I bet you tell every visitor that this old boneyard is haunted.'

Needle-sharp Martin grinned and winked back at me, 'I suppose my mother told you that no one walks in St Jude's graveyard after dark on July 21st.'

Kathy turned her head to laugh at Martin over her shoulder, 'surprise, surprise, that's the date of today. Come off it Martin and pull my other leg – it's got bells on it.'

Martin sounded so sincere when he answered, 'I wouldn't dream of pulling a pretty girl's leg. Kathy would you please read aloud the words on that marble tablet?

Kathy read aloud, 'Emily Westmead 1806-1814 and Sophie Westmead 1802-1814. Drowned in Greenwood Pond on July 21st 1814 – two angels asleep in God's hand.'

Mick stood up and his eyes darted suspiciously at me when he said to Martin. 'Are you trying to tell us that the ghosts of two drowned kids will walk in this graveyard tonight?'

Martin shook his head, 'I've never heard that the Westmead sisters haunt the cemetery.' Martin's voice dropped to a scary whisper, the vicar's teenaged son knew how to spin a good creepy yarn, 'the townspeople keep away from St Jude's cemetery after sunset on July 21st because they don't want to meet Sarah Raith.'

I saw a tiny flicker of belief in Mick's eyes when he demanded in a loud voice, 'who is bleedin' Sarah Raith?'

'Sarah was the Westmead's nanny and she took the sisters to Greenwood Pond to catch tadpoles. They fell into the pond and Sarah couldn't save them because she couldn't swim.'

'What happened to her?' Kathy asked.

'Insane with grief and guilt the poor girl damned her soul by hanging herself from that yew tree that you can see over there growing in the gap in the wall.'

A weathered brick wall that enclosed the church and the cemetery was breached in several places where the passing decades had taken a toll of bricks and mortar. Martin had pointed to a small twiggy tree growing in a gap in the section of the crumbling wall that was between the vicarage vegetable garden and the cemetery. 'Suicides could not be buried in hallowed ground in those days and that space in the wall is as close to consecrated earth as Sarah's corpse could be interred and the yew tree marks her uneasy resting place.'

We could see a runner bean trellis on the other side of the yew tree.

Martin's voice sounded creepily hollow,'it is said that

at the first stroke of midnight on July 21st Sarah drifts among the graves searching for the young sisters' grave. Folk who've seen her in the moonlight say that the long white hanging cord is still around her neck.'

Kathy of course empathised with the ghostly nursemaid, 'it wasn't the poor nanny's fault those kids drowned. They were old enough to know better than to fall into a pond. It's like if you drowned Mick because you did something stupid...like if you tried to go boating on a canal in a busted bassinet pram when you know you can't swim.'

'Thanks a cartload!' Mick muttered but he was too busy digesting Martin's story to have an argument with Kathy.

I threw fuel on Martin's ghost-fire when I loudly sang, 'come out, Sarah Raith, come out wherever you are, Michael Doherty wants to say hello to you.'

'Shut it, Nell.' Mick whispered fiercely as he looked around the sunlit graves, 'stop taking the piss…something might be listening. Not that I'm scared mind you.'

'Well I don't believe that Martin's spooky nursemaid will walk in this bone-yard tonight and I dare you to meet me here at midnight – unless you're too chicken of course.'

Martin backed me, 'don't let the chaps' side down Mick – take up Nell's dare.'

I'd left Mick nowhere to run to save face and he implored me as he pointed at Kathy. 'We can't leave Kathy on her own...not without one of us with her.'

I ruthlessly continued to press the attack home, 'Kathy comes with us as a witness. Don't forget my compass is yours if Sarah appears but of course if Sarah's a no-show you'll agree that ghosts don't exist – in writing.'

Swept along on the crest of his success the vicar's son almost fell overboard. 'If you do go ghost hunting here tonight don't enter the graveyard through the lichgate. Lich is an old name for a corpse and the dead are carried through the corpse-gate...'

Mick's freckles visibly darkened as his face paled and Martin caught my warning head shake in time to hastily add, '...I'm kidding the girls, Mick.'

Mick wasn't reassured.

Martin glanced at his watch, 'this has been fun but I have to scoot, my folks are throwing a dinner party tonight and I've copped the usual chores. Have a safe trip back to London tomorrow and have spooky fun here tonight.' He tipped me a knowing wink before he headed for the break in the wall and the vicarage vegetable garden.

I saw Mick wince when the vicar's son stepped on the nursemaid's supposed grave when he walked through the gap in the broken wall where the yew tree was growing and I made no comment when Mick insisted on leading Kathy and me out of the cemetery and he made a point of leading us through one of the gaps in the crumbling wall even though to exit through the lichgate would have been quicker and easier.

For the rest of that evening I operated upon Mick's oversized male pride and his lust for my pocket compass until a few minutes before the boys were banished to their hut for the night he capitulated and reluctantly accepted my dare to go on a ghost hunt. He agreed, albeit reluctantly, to rendezvous with Kathy and me outside the cemetery lichgate at midnight. We had reached consensus that a half hour vigil in St Jude's graveyard would be sufficient time to establish the reality or the unreality of the spectral nanny.

Kathy swore that we were the most dangerously

stupid best friends in the world and she refused to join the ghost hunt as an impartial observer until she had made Mick and me swear by every vow that we knew and one that Mick claimed Kathy had invented that one of us would be at her side for every second we were inside the graveyard. Kathy had a touching trust in Mick and me but she still insisted on having control of our only light source – a small black-out torch dimmed with blue paper.

I looked forward to the witching hour although sneaking out of the girls' hut window in our nightgowns without waking the chaperones was not the easiest part of the ghost safari. We had chosen to wear nightgowns in case we were caught by one of the W.V.S. minders out of our bunks. We planned to say that Kathy was sleep-walking and that I was coaxing her back to bed – we would have a problem explaining day-clothes in the middle of the night.

Our bright idea of ghost-hunting in our nightwear backfired some when we were caught in a brief heavy rain shower as we were crossing the road. The shower stopped as quickly as it started but our nightgowns were drenched by the time we reached Mick who was dry having bravely sheltered under the lichgate roof.

Mick looked tense and pale in the uncertain moonlight and he kept his back turned to the shadowed leafy tunnel that stretched from the lichgate to the church doors and we followed him when he walked along the crumbling wall until he came to a wide gap. Mick took a deep breath and stepped into the graveyard through the gap in the wall.

I felt uncomfortable not telling Kathy about my secret collusion with Martin but I didn't want to lose this rare opportunity to cure Mick of his illogical occult beliefs. Kathy was so transparent and honest she would have inadvertently have given my game away to Mick.

As we walked through the space in the wall a full moon sailed out from behind a bank of dark cloud into a patch of starry night sky. The pale lunar light revealed knee-high mist rising between the crazily tilted headstones. I led the way to the middle of the graves.

Mick was walking closely behind Kathy and he stopped and unbuttoned his bomber jacket when he noticed her shivering in her wet nightgown.

'When will you two ever think to bring your coats? I swear that both of you have worn my coat more times…' Mick fell silent and raised his right hand...his forefinger pointing ahead.

Kathy gasped and I looked to see what Mick was pointing at and I didn't believe my eyes. A tall woman dressed in a long dark gown stood motionless in the shadow of the yew-tree that Martin said marked Sarah Raith's resting place and when the woman turned her head and stared at us her eyes shone silver in the moonlight.

The woman appeared to float between the misty headstones as Martin's voice replayed in my head, "Sarah drifts between the graves searching for the grave of the young sisters."

Martin! Of course it was the likely lad taking the haunting lark a tad too far but the spectre continued to drift through the graves towards us until even my mulish logic conceded that the ghostly lady staring at us across the grave of the unfortunate Westmead children was not the vicar's son wearing his mother's dress.

Kathy and I clung to each other shivering with

fear. We were as incapable of speech or movement as the stone angel sitting by the grave was of rising and speaking. There was an ominous silence at our backs. I cast a quick glance over my shoulder and the situation was as I feared, Mick had bolted and Kathy and I were alone with the ghostly nanny sadly watching us across the grave of her two drowned children.

Our fear intensified when Sarah opened her arms as if to embrace us but before she could step across the grave a miracle saved us...a quavering falsetto voice began reciting the Roman Catholic Calendar of Saints. I should have trusted Mick to never desert us.

Sarah Raith lifted her head to listen to the litany of holy names and I saw a long white cord hanging around her neck and that was when my battered logic lost its' grip and tumbled from my shoulders. Two more miracles occurred simultaneously, a distant town clock chimed the midnight hour and a black curtain of rain cloud closed off the shining face of the moon.

We fled in the blessed darkness and terror winged us through the dreaded lichgate across the road and up into the open windows of our huts. I surrendered my pocket compass to Mick on the coach ride back to London. I never saw the compass again but the tale of the spectral nurse maid did not finish in 1945...

A spooky twist in 1949…

After the scary night in St Jude's haunted graveyard I believed in the impossible until four years later when I attended a friend's wedding in the Spring of 1949 and a strange twist of fate returned my sensible logic to its' secure perch on my shoulder once again.

At the wedding reception I was seated at the same

table as the bride's aunt who had many interesting stories to tell about her service in the Women's Land Army during the war years and as the evening progressed and the champagne flowed amusing anecdotes about the war began to be told by other guests around the table. I was only seventeen in the spring of 1949 and apart from one small glass of champagne to toast the happy couple I was restricted to drinking soft drinks. I don't recall how a guest's anecdote changed from a hilarious caper in the Home Guard to a supernatural encounter but guests at the table sat up and listened when the bride's aunt spoke in a loud positive voice to her nephew who sat facing her across the table, 'Tell me why should I doubt the reality of ghosts, David.'

'It's rubbish, Aunty.' David grinned and I knew logic was perched on his shoulder.

Good humoured banter erupted between sceptics and believers around the table. I was in the aunt's camp and I was pleased when she finally gave in to the curious guests who were urging her to tell her ghost experience. There was silence when the aunt began her story.

'I had always doubted the reality of ghosts until July 21st 1943. I was working on a small farm in the Chilterns at the time. I was returning to my billet a few minutes before midnight after attending a dinner-party when I took a shortcut through a small graveyard …'

I thought it was my involuntary gasp that had stopped the aunt telling her tale but she was glaring at her nephew who had sniggered. His aunt said curtly, 'don't forget David that there was a war going on. The dinner-party was held at the vicarage and light home-made wine was served with the meal.'

The nephew had the grace to look abashed, 'I'm

sorry Aunty; I wasn't suggesting that you were squiffy but it would be easy to miss-remember the events of an evening four years ago.'

'I recall every detail of that evening. I wore a long evening skirt of royal blue taffeta, black suede shoes with medium heels and a long strand of white coral beads but if you are going to be combative and rude, David…'

I pleaded, 'please go on. I really do want to hear your story.'

The aunt gave me a look of approval and resumed her ghostly tale, 'as I said before I was interrupted, the date was July 21st and that date proved significant later.' She paused to cock her eye-brow at Doubting David but he wisely kept quiet and his aunt continued, 'I thanked the vicar and his wife for a pleasant evening when left the vicarage ten minutes or so before midnight. I declined offers of a lift home it was a lovely moonlit night and I chose to walk. The farm where I was billeted was less than a half mile away if one took a short-cut through a small graveyard that was next-door to the vicarage garden.'

'You walked alone through a graveyard at midnight?' David asked with genuine respect.

'At that time I was like you David, I had no belief in ghosts and saw nothing to fear in walking through a cemetery where no one had been laid to rest for more than half a century. The low brick wall that enclosed the cemetery was crumbling and the moon was illuminating several large gaps where I could enter the graveyard without risk of soiling my long evening skirt. I negotiated a path through the vicarage veggie garden to a wide space in the wall.'

The bride's aunt had obviously told her story before.

She paused for effect and took a sip of champagne before she continued.

'A ground mist common to the area was knee-high and it wasn't until I looked for a safe path through the misty moonlit graves that I saw the ghosts of the two young girls standing beside the statue of a sitting stone angel in the middle of the graveyard.'

Guests at the table gasped and somebody said, 'I would have died of fright.'

I was stunned into silence by the knowledge that Kathy, Mick and I had fled in terror from this fearless flesh and blood ex-Land Army lady who had mistaken us for the dead Westmead children. I asked in a high pitched squeak, 'could mist and moonlight have confused you?'

The bride's aunt smiled kindly at me, 'I'm not that easy to confuse my dear. I am quite certain that in that ancient moonlit cemetery I saw the phantoms of two young girls standing beside a stone statue of a sitting angel and I'm just as certain that the wraiths could see me. The smaller girl had large blue eyes and shoulder-length golden curls. The bigger girl's hair hung to her waist in two thick brown plaits and their long white dresses were water-sodden, that, like the date July 21st, turned out to be another significant factor'

Doubting Dave was not only persistent he became annoying,'you have a cracker of a wild imagination Aunty.'

David's companion said, 'put a sock in it Dave. I want to hear Aunty's story.'

I urged, 'yes, please finish your story – weren't you scared?'

'Not a bit. The sad little creatures were obviously terrified of me.'

'What happened next Aunty?' asked David's companion.

'The strangest event of the evening occurred next . A disembodied voice began chanting the names of the saints as a distant town hall clock chimed the midnight hour. I will hear that angelic holy chanting until the day I die and that wasn't the finish of the night's strangeness.'

Even Dave was hooked, 'what weird stuff happened next?'

'Rain clouds covered the face of the moon and when darkness cloaked the graveyard the chanting ceased. The full moon emerged from behind the dark clouds a minute or so later and the wraiths had vanished. I sat beside the stone angel until the sun rose but there were no further manifestations.'

I had to ask, 'did you tell the vicar about seeing ghosts of children in the graveyard?'

'Yes, I called on the vicar and his wife the next day and they were perplexed. They had lived next-door to the small cemetery for decades without ever suspecting that it was haunted. The vicar accompanied me and we inspected the double grave watched over by the sitting stone angel. Do you remember that I mentioned the significance of the water drenched gowns worn by the ghostly girls?'

Mandarin-doll heads nodded silently around the table.

'The vicar researched church records and discovered that the seated stone angel watched over the grave of two young sisters, Emily and Sophie Westmead who died in a drowning tragedy on July 21st 1814. They were eight and twelve years of age when they died.'

Sceptical David just had to fire a final shot at his aunt, 'An angel's voice chanting names of the saints in an ancient Protestant cemetery sounds suss to me. The vicarage and the graveyard clearly belong to the Church of England and Anglicans are not big on the saints. Is it possible that the homemade wine you drank at the vicarage dinner-party was stronger than it tasted Aunty?'

David's partner slapped the back of his head, 'Ignore him Aunty.'

David's aunt eyed him with cold disapproval, 'the vicar has a teenaged son who is much like you David; he asked me if the chanting angelic voice had a Cockney accent.'

I opted out of the noisy conversation that instantly erupted among the guests sitting around the table. I felt a strange sense of loss. Sarah Raith had stalked me for years and looking out for her moon glittered eyes in dark places had been scary fun.

It was my moral duty to inform the bride's aunt that St Jude's ancient burial ground was at peace but when I saw her bright eyes and her flushed homely face as she held centre stage among the wedding guests I could not send her phantom children into oblivion and as for the vicar and his wife I had no doubt that Martin had straightened out any misconceptions they might have with an amusing tale about Kathy, Mick and me.

I never told Mick that the ghost of Sarah Raith had never existed outside of a vicar's son's devilish imagination. Mick had the right to keep the magic and fly up to the moon with his banshee if he so wished. Besides, as my pragmatic logic whispered in my ear, there was no point to winning the old ghost argument because Mick Doherty would have traded off my pocket compass years ago.

15

1945
cruel Valentine

War had slowed the implementation of a Law to raise the school leaving age to fifteen and Mick eagerly looked forward to his fourteenth birthday in September when he could legally leave school and work full-time for his brother Danny who was now a proud licensed street trader in East Lane who owned his own barrow.

A law that had been implemented in 1944 made Secondary School education free and Dad strongly encouraged me to further my education. Kathy wanted to continue her schooling in order to qualify for entry to a nurse training school but her mother had made arrangements for Kathy to start work at her club and train as a club hostess. Gloria saw nursing as low paid servant work for women who were destined to be old maids.

St Valentine's Day fell on a Wednesday in 1945 and because Kathy was taking that day off school for a dental appointment one of her many admirers had slipped a Valentine Day card into her school-bag on Tuesday and when Kathy showed us the card Mick had teased the admirer unmercifully until Kathy scolded him, 'grow up Mick. Are you sure that you'll be old enough to leave school in September? I should ask Danny to give me your job.'

Mick had voiced what I was thinking, 'I wish you would get a job with Dan, you'll be a lot safer selling tomatoes off Dan's barrow than you'll be selling booze for Gloria's sleazy boss.'

I was relieved when Kathy answered, 'I don't care what Mum plans for me. I'll never go to work for that creepy spiv. My dental appointment on Wednesday is a lie Mum told to get me off school tomorrow. I'm supposed to tidy the flat, fix a nice lunch and look pretty when she brings her boss home to talk over a job at the club for me.'

Kathy spotted the look that passed between Mick and me, 'I didn't tell you two because I knew that you would make a big fuss. Don't worry, I've already had a word with Gran and she's agreed to come upstairs and join us for lunch.'

'Telling Gran was good thinking Kathy,' Mick said, 'I bet Gran will sort out your Mum's sleazy boss and I'll wag school tomorrow afternoon and hang about on your balcony.'

Kathy hugged Mick and shook her head, 'thank you big brother but I'll be safe enough with Gran. If you two must act like mother hens why don't you worry for Paddy? He had a rotten dose of flu when we saw him last Sunday. I wish that he still lived by the canal. Waite Street is too far away for us to keep a proper eye on him. I knew that Mum planned for me to stay home from school on Valentine's Day and when we saw Paddy last Sunday I promised him that I'd manage a brief early visit on Wednesmorning and he asked if I could bring him a pie and mash from the eel shop, I can do that – he said he missed his Friday fish and chips.'

Mick nodded, 'I'll take him a fillet of rock salmon and chips this Friday.'

I had an idea. 'When you see Paddy tomorrow tell him why your mother wants you to leave school. He's a wise old codger and he might come up with an good idea.'

Mick scowled, 'and you tell us if Gloria's boy-friend bothers you tomorrow. He'll think a bleeding V2 has dropped on his fancy club when Danny and I have finished with him.'

I shivered with an ominous chill when Mick lightly mentioned the V2 rocket. The V2 flew through the stratosphere at 3,000 miles an hour and air-raid sirens did not have time to alert the intended victims. The roar of the V.2 engine and the sonic boom were not heard until after a devastating explosion had flattened an entire street. Mick's aunt had been one of the 168 shoppers killed when a V2 devastated the big Woolworths store in New Cross four weeks before last Christmas.

The V1 rockets had come at the start of 1944. Warning sirens sounded whenever a V1 got past the coastal defences and when the loud droning engine of a low flying VI cut out people on the ground had enough time to take cover before the unmanned bomb fell out of the sky and exploded. Anti-aircraft guns, barrage balloons, fighter planes and radar, were all useless defences against the V2.

We nicknamed the V1 rockets buzz-bombs and doodle-bugs. We never coined a nickname for the terrible V2.

When Kathy, Mick and I woke on Wednesday

morning we had no intimation that we were about to experience the darkest St Valentine's Day of our lives.

Mick and I were standing in morning assembly at Sumner Road School on Wednesday 14th February while Kathy was riding her bicycle to Waite Street. Kathy's front basket was loaded with a china bowl filled with pie and mash from Manze's eel shop in Peckham Hill Street, an enamel pint jug half filled with Manze's special tasty parsley liquor, a small jar of Maureen's home-made sloe jam, a dozen scones that I had baked and a large bottle of Gran's potent damson wine that was a favourite tipple of both Paddy and Gran.

At the mid-morning break Mick and I went upstairs to the school's rooftop playground where the girls played netball. Maureen baked London's best spicy bread-pudding and she always put extra slices in Mick's school-bag for Kathy and me and when Mick passed me a thick slice of bread-pudding I glimpsed two colourful hand-painted cards smothered with flowers, hearts and cupids in his school bag.

'I can't believe that you got two Valentines – you've got to be pulling my leg.'

'I found them in my bag after Assembly – it's a bit embarrassing really.' Mick grinned, his face a rosy glow under a mass of freckles.

'Chasing after two girls at the same time will earn you a thick ear old son.' I warned.

'I didn't chase them, they chased me. Don't give me that funny look. Why wouldn't girls want to chase after me?' Mick demanded.

'For one thing you're a noisy bossy git and for another thing the black-eye that you're always sporting these days would put any nice girl off – tell me who sent them then?'

Mick tried to sound off-hand, 'I don't know – but the one with the cupids might be from Sally Taylor – the poor little thing fancies me.' Mick's face had grown fiery red.

As I reached for the cards a boom like the loudest clap of thunder rang my ears and the school vibrated. I had heard a similar thunderous sound a few weeks before Christmas.

I looked at Mick and saw the horror that I was feeling reflected in his eyes. I quietly asked him, 'did that sound like a clap of thunder to you?'

Mick grimly shook his head, 'it sounded like the V2 that killed my aunt at New Cross.'

Mick beat me in our scramble to climb on to the top of an air-duct casing. From the higher vantage point we could see over the parapet surrounding the rooftop playground. Nothing out of the ordinary appeared to be happening for two or three minutes then the road outside the school was filled with people running, riding bicycles, driving army jeeps, ambulances and fire-engines with bells ringing and cars marked with ARP and police insignias – everything speeding along Sumner Road. A wide dark column of smoke was rising from somewhere past the intersection of Sumner Road with Commercial Way and I was cold with fear.

I asked Mick, 'do you think that Kathy is still at Waite Street?'

'I forgot Kathy!' Mick yelled and he jumped off the skylight cover and as he ran to the door to the stairs he yelled back over his shoulder at me, 'go home and get your bike. Wait for me on the corner outside the pub.'

For once I was happy to allow Mick to take charge.

The two monitors policing the school gates made no

attempt to prevent us leaving – Mick had grown a lot larger during the past year.

It was almost half-past eleven when Mick and I met outside the *Alliance* with our bikes. People were rushing past us on their way down Sumner Road, a couple of men sped past on roller skates. Mick and I hitched a fast ride holding on to the back of a speeding ambulance until the ambulance crossed Commercial Way and drove into a thick pall of dust and smoke where Sumner Road merges into Trafalgar Avenue.

The column of smoke that we had seen from the school roof was coming from houses on fire in Trafalgar Avenue. The ambulance slowed and braked at the start of Waite Street and Mick and I dismounted from our bikes in shocked silence.

Paddy's lodging house had been among the first twelve or so tall houses in Waite Street that had vanished. The deep crater that now yawned where the houses once stood was at least forty feet across. The remainder of the houses in the short street were ruined and most were smashed flat.

Mick and I left our bikes on a heap of rubble and nobody tried to stop us when we walked to the edge of the deep crater. The ARP and the police were half-hearted in their efforts to stop frantic people searching through the unsafe ruins of what was left of the Waite Street houses. Searchers were shouting the names of friends and relatives feared buried under the debris and none of the adults challenged our presence in the noisy dusty chaos.

Mick and I watched a police dog handler working with a large Alsatian dog. Guided by the dog's barks and whimpers the policeman brought a dazed bleeding woman and her two small crying children covered in dust out from underneath the rubble of their house. The mother was put on a stretcher and the tearful children were carried by ARP wardens to where doctors in white coats assisted by hospital nurses were administering first-aid. Ambulances waited in lines to ferry the seriously injured to hospital. A large panel van in the ambulance queue had the words Friends Ambulance Unit painted on the side and two quiet men wearing Quaker armbands were gently lifting sheeted shapes on stretchers into the large panel van.

'Kathy left Waite Street before the V2 hit.' Mick suddenly said in a loud aggressive voice and as if challenging me to argue he gripped my arm and pulled me up on to my feet. 'Get your bike. We're going home right now because Kathy ain't here she's waiting for us back at the flats and she needs us.'

I knew Mick was wrong but I didn't answer; I was as incapable of speech or movement as the cracked block of stone upon which I had sat when my shaky legs gave way.

Mick was dragging me towards our bicycles. Dr Cohen's quiet voice close behind us was so unexpected that Mick released his painful grip on my arm.

'That's quite enough, Mick. Kathy isn't waiting for you and Nell back at the buildings as you very well know.'

Dr Cohen's white coat was dusty and bloodstained and he looked exhausted, 'I believe that you and Nell should hear the truth about what happened when the V2 hit Waite Street without warning. Kathy and Mr Kelly died instantly and I swear to you that they did not suffer. I have made arrangements for a church minister to call on Mrs Henson.'

Mick had grown as tall as Dr Cohen and I was only

a head shorter but Dr Cohen gathered us into his arms and held us tight against this chest as if we were small children. I heard Mick Doherty cry for the first time that day and I cried with him. When our tears stopped Dr Cohen released us and stood back. He rested his hands on our shoulders and said in a serious voice, 'I know you don't need a lot of sympathy talk right now about being brave but please believe me when I tell you that the terrible pain you're feeling at this moment will fade and you'll be left with only the memories of your happy times with Kathy and Mr Kelly but that can only happen if you are not afraid to remember and talk about the happy times you've had. Believe me when I tell you that one day you will be happy again.'

Mick reached across and took my damp hanky.

'Make sure you give that back Mick Doherty – you've had too many of my hankies.'

Mick snorted into the embroidered square of linen I'd made from one of Dad's old shirts.

'Yuk! On seconds thoughts you can keep the flaming thing.'

Dr Cohen's eyes were suspiciously bright when he said, 'I want you both to go home now. Don't ride your bikes but walk together because you're both in shock.'

He lightly punched Mick's arm, 'I know that I can trust you old chap to see Nell safely home right to her front door.'

Mick nodded, 'I'll take care of her and don't you worry about us Doc, we'll be okay about Kathy and Paddy – as my Gran says: God's in His Heaven, All's Right with the World.'

I exploded and screamed, 'I'm not okay about Kathy and Paddy and I don't need to be taken care of Mick

Doherty. I've never believed in Heaven and after today I'm not going to believe in bleeding God anymore.'

My outburst stunned me as well as both of them and I stormed away in an embarrassing fresh flood of tears.

'Nell come back!' Mick and Dr Cohen shouted after me with one voice.

I was being rude but I didn't care. I had lost Kathy and I had to strike at someone. Mick and I wheeled our bikes home in silence after I tried to ride but was shaking so hard that I fell off and grazed my elbow, in any case the traffic chaos on Sumner Road made riding a bike too dangerous. A light rain was drizzling when we walked into Bude House square and Mick wheeled his bike in front of me and said earnestly, 'let me carry your bike upstairs to your flat today and I promise that I'll let you carry my bike up to the top balcony of my building tomorrow – twice.' Mick then cringed from me in exaggerated pretence fear.' Don't hit me Nell – I'll tell old Gran on you if you make me cry.'

I squeezed his arm in silent gratitude. Mick had succeeded in making me smile when I was sure that I would never smile again and it was time to repair a very important bridge between me and the boy who was as dear to me as a natural brother.

'Before I let you tote my bike upstairs let's sit under our tree and talk for a bit.'

Mick looked relieved when he nodded agreement. We wheeled our bikes into the stair well entrance out of the rain before we sat close together in the shelter of the tall green friend we used to talk to when we first moved into the buildings and we told our sad news to our tree and Dr Cohen was right, when we reminisced about Kathy and Paddy we felt comforted.

'Mick, do you remember that day during the Blitz when we explored the bombed church on Commercial Way? Kathy found little blue flowers growing in the rubble of the smashed altar and an old A.R.P warden caught us in there.'

Mick grinned, 'I remember the clip over the ear I copped for giving him cheek but the old grouch turned out okay in the end didn't he? He let Kathy pick the flowers and take a bunch of them home.'

I nodded, 'he told us that the church was ancient and that the seeds of the blue flowers had been buried beneath the marble altar for over two hundred years and when the bomb smashed the altar the sun and rain brought the flower seeds back to life. I didn't understand at the time what he was telling us but now I think I do understand.'

'Well I don't. What are you saying?'

'I'm saying that the old ARP warden told us that nothing ever truly dies. I'm also saying that I'm sorry I raved at you and the Doc and I hope with all my heart that you're right and that God and Heaven are real and that Kathy and Paddy are waiting for us in Heaven.'

Mick whispered, 'they'll be there but I hope that you cut down on the waterworks when we all meet in Heaven.'

The tree shed a few more of its' remaining leaves and Mick grinned when he said, 'now look what you've done, you've made our bleeding tree cry too. '

I hugged him, 'have you noticed that we're getting wet, Mick?'

We were both soaked. The light drizzle had become a downpour while we talked and the tree's almost leafless branches offered little protection from heavy rain.

I glimpsed a pale face in the window of a ground-floor flat. The old busy-body and gossip of Bude House was spying on us.

'Mother Huntley is watching us. When she sees my Dad she'll probably tell him that she wouldn't like him to think she is interfering but she thinks he should know that his daughter was cuddling the red-haired Doherty lout in the middle of the square.'

'Doesn't old Mother Nosey Parker know that it's St Valentine's Day?' Mick growled as he pulled me up on to my feet, 'Let's get you and that bleeding bike up the stairs.'

'I don't know about you Mick but I've gone right off St Valentine.'

'Me too – I don't think that I'll ever bleeding laugh again Nell.'

Mick balanced my bike on his shoulder and I was close behind him when we started the long climb up to the top balcony. Half-way up I said in a loud voice, 'by the way thanks for your offer to allow me tote your bike up to the top balcony of your building…twice I think you said. Well I'll tell you now Michael Doherty that will only happen in your dreams.'

When I heard a muffled snort I knew that someday Mick would laugh again.

16

four aftermaths of the war

War in Europe ended three months after the V2 rocket stole the lives of Kathy Henson and Paddy Kelly on St Valentine's Day 1945. War in the Pacific ended in August 1945 shortly after atomic bombs were dropped on two Japanese cities.

1...First Anniversary Fly-past of the Battle of Britain

The first anniversary fly-past of the Battle of Britain was scheduled to pass directly over Peckham on Saturday the 15th of September 1945. I was in the crowd of eager spectators that thronged Peckham High Street to watch the historic event. Vampire jet fighters had been built too late to see combat in the war and the rumour that a squadron of the new jet fighters were going to play a prominent role in the fly-past heightened curiosity in the crowd but it was the Spitfires that most people waited to see and applaud. Mick wasn't with me. Saturday is a busy day for barrow traders and Mick was in East Lane selling fruit and vegetables.

Excitement in the crowd began to build at the distant growl of 300 massed aircraft engines and when a single aircraft appeared overhead people went wild. The lone plane was followed seconds later by a squadron of the thunderous new Vampire jet fighters.

The jet-planes of future wars were leading a 'V" for victory formation of three hundred wartime aircraft but it is the image of that solitary leading plane flying high above the Jones and Higgins clock tower that is permanently engraved on my memory. I heard that Tin-Legs Douglas Bader flew the lone plane that led the 300 planes in the fly-past. I have never been able to confirm this.

2...the Tree in Bude House Square...

The tree in Bude House square was missing in a black and white photograph taken in the late 1970s, chopped down to create more parking spaces for cars. The tree in Bude House square had survived social housing estate planners, incendiary fires and bomb blasts only to be felled by the modern motor car...Vale old green friend.

3... urban renewal of Peckham

Peckham underwent intense urban redevelopment in the 1980s and 1990s. The Sumner Road Social Housing Estate of five storied blocks of cramped flats was eradicated and has been replaced with grass, trees and family friendly housing...pets are permitted.

4...the Peckham Off-Shoot of the Grand Surrey Canal

The canal that ran behind the back fences of the Stanton Street houses was filled in and transformed into a tree-lined walk-way about the same time as the ugly blocks of flats on the Sumner Road Housing Estate were eradicated.

The green walkway begins at the Peckham Library Square and follows the route of the old canal until it reaches lovely Burgess Park and rebuilt Waite Street.

Paddy Kelly our dearly loved Irish story-teller had greatly missed the canal when he was moved to Waite Street after the UXB exploded and destroyed his lodging house although I am sure he would have approved of the canal's final end as a pleasant green walkway.

17

1948
the remembrance poppies were blood-red

Sunday Remembrance service at the Cenotaph on November 14th 1948 was the last that my father and I attended together. On our way to the Cenotaph in Whitehall we detoured to Westminster Abbey to admire the green north lawn that had been transformed into a poignant Field of Remembrance.

When we arrived at the beautiful abbey veterans of the Royal British Legion were doing a brisk trade selling red poppies stapled to small white crosses for planting in the north lawn in memory of the war dead. Dad had lost friends in both world wars on both sides and he bought several crosses. I brought just three, one for Kathy, one for Paddy and one for Granny Gold's granddaughter Katrina and I printed a name on each white cross with a soft black pencil.

'The blood-red poppies of war,' Dad sadly sighed as he contemplated a sea of red poppies on the green lawn front of Westminster Abbey and he had limped back to the poppy sellers to buy two extra crosses. He printed a name neatly on each cross and then he asked me to push them into the green lawn for him.

The names that my father printed on the two crosses were: Hiroshima and Nagasaki.

The End

'There never was a good war or a bad peace.'...Benjamin Franklin.

Lightning Source UK Ltd.
Milton Keynes UK
UKOW02f0615171116
287833UK00001B/20/P

9 780987 212245